ENVIRONMENTAL PHILOSOPHY IN DESPERATE TIMES

T0274935

ENVIRONMENTAL PHILOSOPHY IN DESPERATE TIMES

JUSTIN PACK

broadview press

BROADVIEW PRESS – www.broadviewpress.com
Peterborough, Ontario, Canada

Founded in 1985, Broadview Press remains a wholly independent publishing house. Broadview's focus is on academic publishing; our titles are accessible to university and college students as well as scholars and general readers. With over 800 titles in print, Broadview has become a leading international publisher in the humanities, with world-wide distribution. Broadview is committed to environmentally responsible publishing and fair business practices.

© 2022 Justin Pack

Library and Archives Canada Cataloguing in Publication

Title: Environmental philosophy in desperate times / Justin Pack.
Names: Pack, Justin, 1980- author.
Description: Includes bibliographical references and index.
Identifiers: Canadiana (print) 20220275165 | Canadiana (ebook) 2022027519X | ISBN
    9781554815364 (softcover) | ISBN 9781770488663 (PDF) | ISBN 9781460408025 (EPUB)
Subjects: LCSH: Environmental ethics. | LCSH: Human ecology. | LCSH: Human ecology—Philosophy. |
    LCSH: Environmentalism—Philosophy.
Classification: LCC GE42 .P33 2022 I DDC 179/.1—dc23

Broadview Press handles its own distribution in North America:
PO Box 1243, Peterborough, Ontario K9J 7H5, Canada
555 Riverwalk Parkway, Tonawanda, NY 14150, USA
Tel: (705) 743-8990; Fax: (705) 743-8353
email: customerservice@broadviewpress.com

For all territories outside of North America, distribution is handled by Eurospan Group.

Broadview Press acknowledges the financial support of the Government of Canada for our publishing activities.

Canada

Edited by Alicia Hibbert and Michel Pharand

Book design by Chris Rowat Design

PRINTED IN CANADA

CONTENTS

Introduction   11

SECTION 1   THE DEATH OF THE COSMOS   15

Chapter 1   Native American Metaphysics, Epistemology, and Ethics
             According to Deloria and Wildcat   19
             1.1 Native American Metaphysics   21
             1.2 Native American Epistemology   22
             1.3 Native American Ethics   23
             1.4 Western Metaphysics and Science   24
             1.5 Western Technology   26
             1.6 Deloria's Claim for the Superiority of Indigenous
                  Traditions   27
             1.7 Questions for Discussion   28
             1.8 Further Reading   28

Chapter 2   The Cosmos in Western Thought   31
             2.1 The Metaphysical Structure of the Cosmos   32
             2.2 Ethics and Human Nature in the Timaean Cosmos   33
             2.3 Contemplate the Cosmos   34
             2.4 The Discovery of the Universe and the Death of the
                  Cosmos   35
             2.5 A New Ethics for a New Universe   37
             2.6 Questions for Discussion   38
             2.7 Further Reading   38

Chapter 3   The Death of Nature   41
    3.1   The World as Organism   41
    3.2   Nature as Female   43
    3.3   Nature as Disorder   44
    3.4   The Mechanical Order   45
    3.5   The Death of Nature   46
    3.6   Progress?   47
    3.7   Questions for Discussion   49
    3.8   Further Reading   49

Chapter 4   Religion and the Environment   51
    4.1   Science vs. Religion   52
    4.2   The Historical Roots of Our Ecological Crisis   54
    4.3   Implications   56
    4.4   Questions for Discussion   57
    4.5   Further Reading   58

SECTION 2   ENVIRONMENTAL THEORIES   59

Chapter 5   Deep Ecology   61
    5.1   Against the Dominant Paradigm   61
    5.2   Shallow vs. Deep Ecology   62
    5.3   Going Deeper, Looking for Alternatives   63
    5.4   Principles of Deep Ecology   64
    5.5   Spirituality   66
    5.6   Deep Ecology and Ecocentrism   67
    5.7   Questions for Discussion   67
    5.8   Further Reading   67

Chapter 6   Ecocentrism and the Wilderness Debate   69
    6.1   Aldo Leopold and the Land Ethic   69
    6.2   Ecocentrism   70
    6.3   The Wilderness Debate and the Problem of Colonialism   72
    6.4   Assessing Deep Ecology and Ecocentrism   75
    6.5   Questions for Discussion   77
    6.6   Further Reading   77

Chapter 7   Ecofeminism   79

7.1   Feminisms   79

7.2   Standpoint Theory   81

7.3   Ecofeminism: Against Domination, Toward Care   82

7.4   Criticisms   84

7.5   Questions for Discussion   85

7.6   Further Reading   86

Chapter 8   Bioregionalism   89

8.1   What Is a Bioregion?   89

8.2   Dwellers in the Land   91

8.3   The Politics of Bioregionalism   92

8.4   Opting Out: Radical Homemaking   93

8.5   Concerns about Bioregionalism   93

8.6   Eating and Living Locally   94

8.7   Questions for Discussion   94

8.8   Further Reading   94

SECTION 3   ENVIRONMENTAL MOVEMENTS   97

Chapter 9   Food Ethics   99

9.1   Vegetarianism   99

9.2   The Industrialization of Eating   101

9.3   Farming and Labor   103

9.4   CAFOs   104

9.5   Slow Food   104

9.6   Intersectionality and Food   105

9.7   Questions for Discussion   106

9.8   Further Reading   107

Chapter 10   Animal Liberation and Mass Extinction   109

10.1   Animal Liberation   109

10.2   Animal Liberation vs. Environmental Ethics   112

10.3   Animal Liberation vs. Animal Rights   112

10.4   The Sixth Mass Extinction   113

10.5   Questions for Discussion   114

10.6   Further Reading   115

Chapter 11   The Climate Change Movement 117
      11.1   Antecedents to the Environmental Movement 117
      11.2   The Environmental Movement 118
      11.3   Climate Change 119
      11.4   Getting Involved 121
      11.5   Questions for Discussion 122
      11.6   Further Reading 122

SECTION 4   WHY ARE WE NOT DOING MORE? 125

Chapter 12   Climate Denial 129
      12.1   The Issues 129
      12.2   Why Support Cigarette Companies and Oppose
            Environmental Regulations? 130
      12.3   The Methods of Denial 132
      12.4   From Doubt to Outright Lies 133
      12.5   A Note on Arguing about Reality and Facts 134
      12.6   Against Environmentalism 135
      12.7   Questions for Discussion 136
      12.8   Further Reading 136

Chapter 13   Epistemology of Ignorance and the Environmental Crisis 137
      13.1   Epistemologies of Ignorance 138
      13.2   Terracide without Biophobia 140
      13.3   Questions for Discussion 142
      13.4   Further Reading 142

Chapter 14   Modern Myths: Economism and Progress 145
      14.1   Economism 146
      14.2   The Myth of Progress 148
      14.3   Modern Identity: Freedom, Dignity, and Power 150
      14.4   Questions for Discussion 151
      14.5   Further Reading 151

Chapter 15 Thoughtlessness and the Environmental Crisis 153

    15.1 Arendt on Thinking and Thoughtlessness 153

    15.2 Eichmann 155

    15.3 Milgram's Shock Box 156

    15.4 Implications for the Environmental Crisis 158

    15.5 Questions for Discussion 159

    15.6 Further Reading 159

Chapter 16 World Alienation and *Amor Mundi* 161

    16.1 World Alienation 161

    16.2 Overcoming World Alienation: *Amor Mundi* 164

    16.3 Desperate Times 166

    16.4 Questions for Discussion 166

    16.5 Further Reading 167

References 169

Index 175

INTRODUCTION

This book is desperate.

Cheetah, lemur, giraffe, elephant, shark, bird, amphibian, and insect populations are crashing. The Great Barrier Reef is continuously bleaching. Islands of plastic garbage are floating in the ocean and microplastics are appearing unexpectedly in the most far-flung places. We are facing human-caused global warming and mass extinction. In 2018, the UN Intergovernmental Panel on Climate Change warned that as early as 2030 we may hit a tipping point of no return when it comes to global warming—accelerating the potential for drought, flood, wildfires, and food shortages. To stop this catastrophe, we need "rapid, far-reaching and unprecedented changes in all aspects of society."

Despite the need for globally coordinated, institutional responses, however, we find haphazard efforts riddled with confusion, hampered by the active spread of misinformation, climate denial, face-saving, and an entrenched reluctance to do anything that slows the economy. Altogether, these are creating a pervasive and widespread thoughtlessness about the environmental crisis that discourages the necessary radical cultural and institutional changes.

Many of the current environmental ethics and environmental philosophy textbooks (and similar textbooks in other disciplines) are not responding adequately to these challenges. They tend to engage with these complex issues using a traditional philosophical approach that seeks to be "objective" and distanced. That is to say, they often proceed rather coldly through an overview of the major normative theories in ethics and the various traditions within environmental ethics, and present the pros and cons of various environmental debates. Rarely do they address the active spread of misinformation and climate denial, genuinely challenge the economism of modern societies and institutions, or, as a result, adequately express the critical nature of the current crisis.

This is particularly frustrating, given that environmental philosophy is one of the most radical subdisciplines in philosophy and is uniquely poised to confront that crisis.

This text attempts to address the remarkable thoughtlessness and hold of the contemporary status quo by grappling with environmental issues in the context of misinformation, climate denial, institutional inaction, and economism. By invoking climate denial, thoughtlessness, and world alienation, this text foregrounds our failure to think through this dire situation, the forces that deny how desperate the environmental crisis has become, and our disconnection from and failure to love the world. We see thoughtlessness as not merely ignorance, since the scientific facts are clear, but as a complex result of misinformation, myths, delusion, and denial. The situation grows increasingly desperate, as climate denial is not merely the rejection of climate change but has come to include the denial of mass extinction, the destruction and disruption of ecosystems worldwide, and the environmental crisis in general.

This text has four sections. The opening section seeks to disrupt ingrained thoughtlessness by displacing readers through sustained attention to non-Western, non-modern, and feminist critiques, beginning with eye-opening critiques from Native American authors Vine Deloria Jr. and Daniel Wildcat. This text then traces how the metaphysical assumptions of a tradition shape social and self-identity, epistemology, and ethics by comparing and contrasting Deloria Jr. and Wildcat's Native American ways of knowing and being with contemporary Western understanding and experience. After this opening salvo, this text examines the metaphysics of the premodern Western cosmos, the shift to the modern (mechanical) universe, the ensuing "death of nature," and the implications of these profound changes.

The second section presents key theories in environmental philosophy: deep ecology, ecocentrism and the wilderness debate, ecofeminism, and bioregionalism. Each of these approaches is complex and multifaceted, have been the topic of individual full-length studies, and have seen their popularity shift multiple times. None of these approaches is without flaws, but each has challenged us to rethink what we are doing and how we understand the current crisis. They are desperate theories calling for radical change and are presented as such.

The third section presents key movements in environmental philosophy: food ethics, animal liberation and mass extinction, the climate change movement. Environmental philosophy has debated the value of seemingly unending philosophical arguments while real-world issues need resolving. Because the tone of this text is one of desperation, this text may seem intentionally more focused on activism than theory. We need both. We need to think about what we are doing, and we need to act. And in environmental philosophy, theory and activism are often interrelated.

The final section focuses on an urgent question: Why aren't we doing more? There is, and has been for some time, widespread agreement among scientists about the problem of climate change. Yet there seems to be very little change at the levels of both individual behavior and institutional practice. While the sections on environmental theories and movements are typical of an introductory text, this section, like the first, is atypical and will involve more argumentation than the rest of the text. There are chapters on climate denial, epistemic ignorance, economism, myths and narratives of progress, thoughtlessness, and world alienation.

SECTION ONE

THE DEATH OF THE COSMOS

Is there something uniquely dangerous about the current environmental crisis? Humans have caused environmental problems in the past. Ancient humans killed off many of the Ice Age megafauna. Farmers destroyed many of the forests in Europe and Asia long ago. Belligerent warring empires in the classical world caused human and environmental devastation. And yet, there is something different with the rise of modernity.

Modernity is generally taken to be a new period in human history—starting as early as the 1600s or 1700s in some places—in which humans have grown increasingly confident about their ability to understand and alter the world. In fact, modernity is perhaps best understood as a project.[1] The project of modernity is the dream of remaking the world to improve human existence. It is often associated with science, the rise of the modern state,

15

technology, and modern civilizations. The changes involved are so drastic that everything prior to modernity is often labeled "premodern."

Many peoples had modernity imposed on them from the outside, and this imposition occurred in various places at different times. In the United States, for example, the Dawes Act of 1877 told Native Americans that they had to stop living nomadic lifestyles, settle the land, and farm it as Western settlers did, or else the government would remove them and give their land to settlers who would farm it. Later, boarding schools—called 'residential schools' in Canada—were established in North America to "civilize" Indigenous children. The purpose of these schools was to erase Indigenous cultural traditions by teaching children English and also how to act like settlers. In fact, however, this practice caused physical and emotional abuse, malnourishment, death, and the intergenerational trauma that Indigenous Peoples continue to experience today. These actions were colonial impositions of one group upon another. Alarmingly, they were carried out by "progressives" of the time who thought they were helping Native Americans join modern society.

Modernization can also be imposed within a nation's own borders, as with various efforts in Latin America in the 1800s, the Meiji Restoration and modernization of Japan beginning in 1868, and the modernization of European peasants—which occurred at different times in different places in Europe (there were still peasants living "premodern" lives in France and other locations into the 1900s). At present, there are very few peoples and places left in the world that have not been subjected to modernization.

The drivers and advocates of modernization projects worldwide saw or see themselves as "improving" human life through these changes. They point to increases in GDP, health, food security, education, etc. as evidence that life is getting better. These efforts are ongoing.

We cannot hope to understand all the changes involved with the shift to modernity (many lengthy books explore these changes), but there are indeed certain fundamental elements that indicate something unique about the current "modern" environmental crisis as opposed to "premodern" ones. This unit will explore perhaps the most radical change bearing on the relation of humans to their environment: the death of the cosmos.

For most, if not all, premodern societies and cultures, the world around us was considered alive and full of gods. Trees, animals, the wind, goblins, djinns, spirits: life was everywhere.[2] Premodern people had to communicate with all these different beings, establish relationships with them, keep the peace, share, plead, and work with them.[3] The stars above, the gaze of a crow, the path of a snake—all of this was meaningful and deeply important. For many, this was not chaos; rather, as we see in the Greek word *kosmos*, this was order.

But in the modern era we have fundamentally altered how we understand the cosmos. For most people now, it is no longer a living thing. Rather we tend to think of it as the complex interactions of various physical forces, or even as a machine. Whenever I teach this topic, I ask students to write down the first things that come to mind when they hear the word "cosmos." Typically, they write words like "space," "empty," "vast," "cold," "alien," and "infinite." Of the hundreds of students to whom I have asked this question, only one has ever said "home." None have ever said "love."

We now live in the "universe," which comes from the Latin *unum versum* and means something like the "one thing"; in other words, "all the stuff in the big thing." Compared to the living cosmos, the universe is dead. This doesn't mean all the plants and animals are dead, but only that we tend to think of them more like machines than gods. In the universe, much of the world around us has a lesser status than it did to premodern thinkers contemplating the cosmos. You can see this in expressions such as "oh, it's just an animal," "it's just some rocks," or "don't worry, it's just the wind." Some environmentalists have warned that in modernity we act as though only humans matter—everything else is inferior. Other things are good only to the degree that they are useful to humans. To reduce the world around us in this way is to empty it of any inherent dignity, divinity, or meaningful independent life.

As we will see in Chapter 3, Carolyn Merchant argues that we have shifted from thinking of the Earth as our mother to thinking of it as a machine. Of course, this results in a drastic difference in how we relate to the Earth and everything on it. If the Earth or Nature is our mother, then we need to treat her with respect and care. We should be grateful for what she gives us and not force her to do as we wish. Similarly, as we will see in Chapter 1, Vine Deloria Jr. and Daniel Wildcat argue that many Native American traditions have worldviews that differ from the modern conception of the universe as machine. Plants, animals, rocks, and mountains, are seen as older brothers and sisters of humankind and that, as such, we should treat them with respect and seek to learn from them.

Our ethical relationships with the world around us change depending on what we consider the nature of our world to be. If it is our mother or our siblings, we should learn from it and perhaps even love it. If it is a machine, we should fix it and improve it. Our contrasting attitudes toward the world around us emerge from these fundamentally different understandings of its nature.

In modernity, it is not just the scale of human action that has changed. We have killed the cosmos and now treat it as an object to be manipulated and controlled for our benefit. From a premodern perspective, this is a shocking and brutal act, not unlike genocide. And while such a claim will seem overwrought from a modern perspective, this goes a long way toward explaining not only the human-caused mass extinction occurring right now, but also the disturbing lack of concern about it.

This book begins with the death of the cosmos, out of a conviction that understanding what has been lost helps us appreciate the immense ethical weight to our human relationships with the natural world. To take the environmental crisis seriously, we may need to nurture more than ourselves as humans.

We begin in Chapter 1 with Deloria and Wildcat's condemnation of destructive modern practices and defense of Native American traditions. In Chapter 2, we examine Rémi Brague's description of the shift in Western conceptions of the world, from the cosmos to the universe. In Chapter 3 we turn to Merchant's discussion of the shift from Mother Earth to the machine-like Earth. Lastly, we look at Lynn White Jr.'s famous discussion of the role of the Judeo-Christian tradition in shaping attitudes toward the natural world.

Notes

1 Castro Gomez, Santiago. "The Social Sciences, Epistemic Violence and the Problem of the 'Invention of the Other'." *Views from South*, vol. 3, no. 2 (2002), 269–85.

2 Jonas, Hans. *The Phenomenon of Life: Toward a Philosophical Biology* (Evanston, IL: Northwestern University Press, 2001).

3 Wilson, Stephen. *The Magical Universe: Everyday Ritual and Magic in Pre-Modern Europe* (New York: Hambledon and London, 2000).

1

NATIVE AMERICAN METAPHYSICS, EPISTEMOLOGY, AND ETHICS ACCORDING TO DELORIA AND WILDCAT

There is no one better qualified to open this book than Vine Deloria Jr. (1933–2005). Both an academic and an activist, Deloria was the most preeminent voice in Native American philosophy and offers a powerful defense of Indigenous traditions and the living cosmos against the destruction caused by Western "civilization." His influence both among Indigenous and non-Indigenous peoples alike is due in part to his willingness to speak truth to power no matter how shocking or uncomfortable that may seem. To awaken both Indigenous and non-Indigenous peoples, his work flips the tables on Western thought, which, he argues, when it hasn't denigrated Native Americans outright, has spoken *about* them, *over* them, and *for* them. He insists, like the title of his 1970 book, that *We Talk, You Listen*.[1] His writing carries tremendous weight because it is no mere academic exercise: Indigenous cultures and lives are under active threat from Western colonialism, and traditional homelands (including plants, animals, mountains, etc.) and peoples are being destroyed by Western practices. Having been told by science who he is, he will now tell science what it is. Having been told his culture is inferior and primitive, he will now show how Native American traditions are superior to and more ethical than Western ones.

We should listen to him, and we should be aware of some of the tensions involved in discussing Indigenous traditions and practices.

First, there are many Indigenous tribes, cultures, and traditions. Vine Deloria Jr. often speaks in general terms about Native Americans. This is not because he was unaware of the differences among Indigenous peoples. He traveled widely and worked with Indigenous peoples of many different traditions. Rather, his use of generalizations about Native Americans stems from their shared plight in the face of Western colonialism. Deloria also knows that not all Western peoples and Western thought are the same. He is particularly fascinated with Western thinkers who break with the Western tradition. And yet, despite the differences among Native American traditions and those among Western traditions, Deloria will contrast "Native American" metaphysics, epistemology, and ethics with "Western" metaphysics, epistemology, and ethics. Such generalizations inherently involve simplifications and reductions, but they are also necessary to clarifying the key issues at stake in order to defend Native American cultures, peoples, lands, and those lands' nonhuman beings.

Second, there is a long history of non-Indigenous writers demonizing, romanticizing, or using Native Americans for their own profit. One problem here is misrepresentation, whether supposedly positive (like Rousseau's "noble savages") or negative (like "cowboy-and-Indian" movies). Another problem is making use of Native Americans—their customs, traditions, or philosophy—in ways that benefit whites or other groups rather than Native Americans. This could involve selling Native American artwork or music, effecting tourism at sacred sites, or white authors benefiting from Native American stories or philosophy. Native American artists, musicians, and authors might not be able to advance their careers (find a market for or protect their traditions) because they are being crowded out, appropriated by others, or lack a white patron. This dynamic has been especially egregious in academia: Deloria comments that, "without the voices of respected white scholars, there is little chance that we can get sufficient attention from the scientific establishment in order to plead our own case."[2]

This chapter closely follows Vine Deloria Jr. and Daniel Wildcat's *Power and Place: Indian Education in America*, a text written primarily for an Indigenous student readership to encourage a discussion of what "[I]ndigenized, educational practice would look like."[3] Of course Deloria and Wildcat are aware that there will also be a non-Indigenous audience, and for those of us who are not Native American, it is critically important to respect Indigenous sovereignty, seek to avoid misrepresentation and profiting at the expense of Native Americans, and, as Deloria puts it bluntly, to "clean up what they have already screwed up."[4] This chapter may thus encourage readers to engage with the original writings of these and other Indigenous thinkers, to become more aware of the history of colonialism, and to generate better efforts to clean up what has been "screwed up."

1.1 NATIVE AMERICAN METAPHYSICS

Metaphysics deals with the nature of being or reality. To speak of Native American metaphysics is to speak of the Indigenous understanding of the nature of the world. According to Deloria, the key concepts required to understand Native American metaphysics are *power* and *place*:

> ... [P]ower being the living energy that inhabits and/or composes the universe, and place being the relationship of things to each other. It is much easier, in discussing Indian principles, to put these basic ideas into a simple equation: Power and place produce personality. This equation simply means that the universe is alive, but it also contains within it the very important suggestion that the universe is personal and, therefore, must be approached in a personal manner.[5]

For Deloria and Wildcat, the key difference between Native Americans and the West is that, according to Indigenous metaphysics, the universe is alive, while according to Western metaphysics the universe is dead or mechanical. What does it mean to say the universe is alive? What exactly is alive? Not only are plants and animals alive, but rocks, wind, rivers, mountains, and landscapes also. They have power and living energy, and they can affect us. Not only are all these things alive, but Deloria claims that many Native American creation stories portray humans as the last creation. Unlike the Christian origin story of Adam and Eve, which is commonly interpreted as claiming humankind as God's peak creation, Native American creation stories present humans as the younger siblings of those other beings created before we were.[6] As such, we should learn from them and must respect them. These beings include four-legged creatures, beings that fly, spirits, mountains, trees, and rocks.

Thus, the universe is alive and full of power, and humans must respect nonhuman peoples, as they are our older siblings. What does place have to do with this? Place is "the relationship of things to each other." Plants, animals, rocks, rivers, and wind will all act differently based on which other people they are related to in a particular place. The same kind of animal might act differently in one place than in another because of the different peoples comprising different places. The Sonoran Desert is different from the Sierra Nevada mountain range and both are different from coastal redwood forests. A mountain lion will alter some of its behaviors in each place because it must deal with different threats and opportunities. Altogether, the many peoples of a place and the power they bring to it give that place what Deloria calls 'personality'. The coastal redwood forests have a unique personality and feel distinct from the Sonoran Desert. Even the same place can have a very different personality at the heart of winter than at the height of summer. Various and often diverse peoples migrate in and out of certain locations, or flourish at certain times while hibernating or dying off at others. To understand a place and act ethically in that place requires treating each of the many peoples it comprises as persons while responding appropriately to the personalities of both places and peoples.

1.2 NATIVE AMERICAN EPISTEMOLOGY

Epistemology is the study of knowledge or how we gain knowledge. According to Deloria and Wildcat, Native Americans gained knowledge through personal and practical relationships with the peoples of a particular place. These peoples are humans' older siblings and have wisdom that we can learn if we listen to, observe, and interact with them. As such, Native American technologies involve "establishing relationships with the larger cosmic rhythms and following those cycles."[7] This means paying attention to how all the peoples of a place are related. Different places have different growing seasons, soils, fungi, insects, rainfall patterns, migratory birds, or patterns of temperatures that affect when various crops should be planted, growing seasons. Thus to really know a place is a process that might take years, and the knowledge and wisdom gained would be transmitted from one generation to another. This, of course, is why it is important to listen to elders: they carry the knowledge of a particular tradition and respect the sacred rituals that developed in particular contexts.

Here we see why both power and place are important to Indigenous epistemology. Since the peoples of the world are powerful, it is important to respect them. Not doing so could entail death: floods, droughts, dangerous animals, poisonous plants, snowstorms, and diseases all manifest potentially dangerous power. But how much of a potential problem these threats are depends on the dynamics of a particular place. Inversely, if we work with and learn from the peoples of a particular place, we can respond ethically and appropriately to their power. Salmon run, acorns fall, insects reproduce, and edible plants grow at certain times of the year, and knowing where to be, and when and what to do, allows humans to participate in these natural bounties. Knowing what, where, and when to plant also enables human flourishing. This knowledge does not apply to all places and all times, however. On the contrary, it is specifically tied to certain places—and different places require different kinds of knowledge.

1.3 NATIVE AMERICAN ETHICS

Probably the most surprising implication of Indigenous metaphysics from a Western perspective is that ethics is related to place. This makes perfect sense once one understands Native American metaphysics: different places have different peoples interconnected in different ways, which requires different ethics. Acting ethically in the Sonoran Desert is not the same as acting ethically in the coastal redwoods. Furthermore, since ethics is related to place, it must be found and developed in that place. To be clear, ethics is not in our heads or in our hearts: it is in and with the world. Hence Wildcat's claim: "The idea that morality and values cannot be found in nature is one of the single most erroneous notions Western civilization have produced and one of the major reasons American Indians often find science uninviting."[8]

The world is imbued with meaning and ethical imperatives. Learning what is right and acting ethically is something that must occur while interacting with the peoples of a place. That process is informed by tradition and tribal wisdom, which, however, have not been created in a vacuum and have evolved during years of interaction with a place.

As Deloria claims, ethics is personal. It is not a relationship between beings of higher status (humans) and beings of lower status (plants, animals, etc.). On the contrary, since humans are the younger siblings of nonhuman peoples, they must be approached respectfully and personally. Take for example this beautiful passage by Native American biologist Robin Wall Kimmerer about sweetgrass:

> Hold out your hands and let me lay upon them a sheaf of freshly picked sweetgrass, loose and flowing, like newly washed hair. Golden green and glossy above, the stems and banded with purple and white where they meet the ground. Hold the bundle up to your nose, find the fragrance of honeyed vanilla over the scent of river water and black Earth and you understand its scientific name: *Hierochlie odorata*, meaning the fragrant, holy grass. In our language it is called *wiingaashk*, the sweet-smelling hair of Mother Earth. Breathe it in and you start to remember things you didn't know you'd forgotten.[9]

The language here is almost reverential. Don't mistake it for romanticism, however. We don't have to snuggle grizzly bears to recognize and respect them: some peoples need distance. The point is that bears and grass are being treated as persons, not as objects.

Robin Wall Kimmerer has also written poignantly about one of the most seemingly insignificant plants: moss.[10] Combining science with an ethical approach that sees relationships with the natural world as personal, Kimmerer presents moss as fascinating, complex, and wonderful. The effect of drawing attention to what is usually treated as the lowliest plant accentuates not only how much of the world around us we are not seeing (and, as a result, how endangered that world has or can become); but also the richness of the world if we will only listen and see it. Why does Western thought make it so difficult to see the world in this way?

1.4 WESTERN METAPHYSICS AND SCIENCE

According to Deloria and Wildcat, Western metaphysics undermines ethical relations with the world's nonhuman peoples because it strips them of their personhood, leaving them powerless and reduced to physical matter. Wall Kimmerer agrees and points out that her scientific training, which is objective and abstract, often conflicts with her Native American ethics. These authors agree that while modern science is a powerful means of understanding the world's physical or material aspect, it cannot say much about meaning, ethics, or spirituality. The social sciences and the humanities, which cannot avoid these nonphysical aspects of human life, have never been able to formulate methodologies that are as successful as those in the physical sciences. This creates a situation that Vine Deloria Jr. and Daniel Wildcat deem very dangerous: only the physical world can be studied with a strong degree of success, while the spiritual, meaningful, and ethical aspects of human existence—which are the most important—are too often left behind. Hence this claim by Wildcat:

> Let's be clear: certain 'things' can be understood using the metaphysics of time, space and energy [modern science]. However, a great deal of what we experience cannot be explained within the metaphysics of Western science, and that is the critical point. An entire realm of human experience in the world is marginalized, declared unknowable, and, consequently, left out of serious consideration. This reality cannot fit in the objective experimental box of mechanical cause and effect, and no tool or technology will change this situation unless we merely say that all there really is to the world is mechanics (in the structural sense) and tools. Western notions of reality and corresponding ideas of knowledge are not far from this cold 'scientific' assessment.[11]

Wildcat appeals to our everyday experience, which is nothing like the mere physical world described by science. True, there is a physical component to the world around us, but we live in a meaningful, ethically and aesthetically charged world full of friends, family, trees, birds, stories, purpose, frustrations, boredom, love, ugliness, and beauty; we don't experience a world of particles.

Notice that Deloria and Wildcat are not claiming some conspiracy on the part of scientists to silence meaning, ethics, and aesthetics. Rather, the success of science and the profitability of STEM jobs, combined with the relative lack of such success in the social sciences and humanities and the lesser degree of profitability of non-STEM jobs, means that science is epistemologically more prestigious and financially more profitable. Even if scientists stay in their lane and limit themselves to discovering knowledge about the physical world, the ensuing disparity between successful knowledge of the physical world and contested knowledge of meaning, ethics, and aesthetics has tended to diminish the appeal and influence of the non-(hard) sciences. The critical error is to mistake epistemic success for ontological reality; in other words, too often the success of obtaining knowledge about the physical world combined with the difficulty of doing so with regard to meaning, ethics, and aesthetics leads to the conclusion that only the physical world exists and that meaning, ethics, and aesthetics are merely values we bring to the physical world.

A careful scientist should not make these claims (or at least recognize that any such claims are not scientific but philosophical), but Deloria and Wildcat believe that after years of success with regard to the physical world, Western thought has drifted this way. The ironic result, Wildcat claims, is that the primary form of gaining knowledge cannot fully describe the everyday world we experience. The West has fallen prey to a "fallacy of misplaced concreteness" that reduces this complex world to something "disjointed, sterile and emotionless."[12] Stripped of power and personality, the world can be remorselessly altered, used, and commodified. It is reduced to mere things, available for use by humans.

While it is likely that this catastrophic de-personification and reduction of the world is something of an accident, Western "science" has a long history of stepping out of its limits when it comes to Native Americans. For years, Western thinkers have marshaled "science" to claim Native Americans are primitive and inferior. These "scientific" truths have been leveraged for the political purposes of taking Indigenous lands, separating and forcibly "reeducating" Indigenous children, and belittling Indigenous beliefs. Deloria is angry at science, not just because misunderstandings about science have led to a reductive Western metaphysics that justifies predation on the natural world, but because science has repeatedly done the same to Native Americans.

Deloria is not referring only to colonial events in the past. Deloria has railed against anthropologists and archaeologists that continued to dig up Native American graves and holy sites, display Indigenous artifacts as objects of cultural interest for Westerners (first disrupt and destroy; then put on display), and reject Native American accounts of their own past in favor of "scientific" accounts (in particular the claim that Native Americans originate from Asia, having crossed the Bering Strait). Despite its very disturbing track record of racism and eugenics, science wields such cultural authority in the West that many of its abuses are dismissed as aberrations and past mistakes. Deloria claims that Native Americans can only wish that were true.

1.5 WESTERN TECHNOLOGY

Wildcat worries that despite the technological advances brought about by modern science, there are also critical moral losses:

> [Modern] technologies increasingly insulate us from direct experience and the acquisition of experiential knowledge from natural environments.
>
> Automobiles, television, air conditioning, and computers, to pick four obvious examples, result in human convenience, entertainment, comfort and escape from incredible drudgery. But I interact less directly and physically in time and space with other human beings and the natural environment because of the ease, comfort, privacy or relative isolation with which I can use these technologies. Technology, in general, has reshaped most people's everyday lives, often in measurably positive ways. But here is the irony: as we disengage technology from communities [which include plants, animals and the geographic/geologic features] with a sense of place, and thereby create cultures and forms of communication that are relatively abstract, we unconsciously destroy conditions for our human survival and threaten the lives of many other plants and animals with whom we share this biosphere.[13]

Notice that Indigenous technologies are tied to place. Knowing when to plant and how to plant requires knowledge of a specific place: the length of the seasons, rainfall, features of the soil, etc. Modern technologies "liberate" us from the constraints of time and place, allowing us to grow foods in places where they do not grow naturally, during seasons they do not normally grow, and to transport foods to locations where they do not grow at all. The moral effects of this are twofold: first, we become alienated from the environment, increasingly ignorant of the rhythms and cycles of the land and seasons, and accustomed to having whatever we want when we want it; second, we increasingly treat the world and its peoples as fungible objects of our desires. If we want strawberries in November, we will have them; if we want them bigger and redder, we will make them so. To be clear, this is not to say that Native Americans did not cultivate plants and animals and alter them over time, but these activities were limited both morally and practically by place. Whereas there is a connection between morality and place in Indigenous thought, many Western technological practices sever humankind from morality and community. This leads to a state of "technological homelessness."[14]

This alienation from the world cannot be healed by newer and better technologies. It involves a fundamental disjunction in Western self-understanding between the self and place. Deloria claims that when life became out of balance, the whole tribe had to work together to heal this lack of balance.[15] However, when the insatiable consumerism of Western practice combines with a radical alienation from the world, Western culture may not be able to prevent eating the world out from under itself.

1.6 DELORIA'S CLAIM FOR THE SUPERIORITY OF INDIGENOUS TRADITIONS

Remember that Deloria and Wildcat are writing primarily for Indigenous students, many of them facing difficult decisions about their education. They know that "science is often the key to employment" and yet, according to Deloria, "Western science has no moral basis and is entirely incapable of resolving human problems except by the device of making humans act more and more like machines."[16] Ultimately, his hope is that Native American traditions and understanding will restore some humanity to contemporary life through the indigenization of education, politics, and ethics.

At a civil rights fundraiser in the 1960s, Deloria provocatively claimed the following:

> We are fighting for ideological survival. Our ideas will overcome your ideas. We are going to cut the country's whole value system to shreds.
>
> It isn't important that there are only 500,000 of us Indians. What is important is that we have a superior way of life. We Indians have a more human philosophy of life. We Indians will show this country how to act human. Someday this country will revise its constitution, its laws, in terms of human beings, instead of property.[17]

To white or other non-Indigenous readers, these words might appear offensive and dismissive, but Deloria is performing a reversal: talking to white settler culture the way it talked to Native Americans for hundreds of years. Deloria is being deliberately provocative.

In light of our desperate times, however, perhaps such provocation can help shake us up a bit, make us sit up and pay attention. He is concerned not just about Native Americans but also about the many older siblings that are currently threatened by human activity. Wildcat has explicitly connected these issues to the current environmental crisis in his *Red Alert!: Saving the Planet with Indigenous Knowledge*.

Wildcat and Deloria are not the only authors to propose that the current environmental crisis is tied to metaphysics. The next two chapters explore the metaphysics of premodern Western thought and how this thought changed radically with the scientific discovery of the modern universe.

1.7 QUESTIONS FOR DISCUSSION

1. According to Deloria, what is Power? What is Place? How do the concepts of power and place change ethics?
2. What is the difference between Indigenous technology and Western technology? Why does Western technology result in alienation from the world?
3. Why might Native Americans find science uninviting both in terms of (a) the history of science and (b) the practice of science?

1.8 FURTHER READING

In addition to *Power and Place: Indian Education in America*, Deloria has written many other books on a great variety of topics. Wildcat's *Red Alert!: Saving the Planet with Indigenous Knowledge* directly addresses the current environmental crisis. Robin Wall Kimmerer's *Gathering Moss: A Natural and Cultural History of Mosses* compares and contrasts Indigenous practices with science while also trying to help us recover an appreciation for something as "lowly" as moss.

Notes

1 Deloria, Jr., Vine. *We Talk, You Listen: New Tribes, New Turf* (Lincoln, NE: Bison Books, 1997).
2 Deloria, Jr., Vine and Daniel Wildcat. *Power and Place: Indian Education in America* (Golden, CO: Fulcrum, 2001), 5.
3 Ibid., v.

4 Ibid.
5 Ibid., 22–23.
6 Ibid., 60.
7 Ibid., 58.
8 Ibid., 136.
9 Wall Kimmerer, Robin. *Braiding Sweetgrass: Indigenous Wisdom, Scientific Knowledge and the Teaching of Plants* (Minneapolis, MN: Milkweed Editions, 2015), ix.
10 Wall Kimmerer, Robin. *Gathering Moss: A Natural and Cultural History of Mosses* (Corvallis, OR: Oregon State University Press, 2003).
11 Deloria, Jr., Vine and Daniel Wildcat. *Power and Place: Indian Education in America* (Golden, CO: Fulcrum, 2001), 12.
12 Ibid., 2.
13 Ibid., 76.
14 Ibid., 67.
15 Ibid., 63.
16 Ibid., 4.
17 Ibid., 69.

2

THE COSMOS IN WESTERN THOUGHT

This chapter presents Rémi Brague's account of how the cosmos was understood and experienced in premodern Western thought. There exist other similar and perhaps more well-known accounts, such as Alexandre Koyre's classic work *From the Closed World to the Infinite Universe*, but Brague's *The Wisdom of the World* has the virtue of clearly exploring the kinds of connections between metaphysics, epistemology, and ethics that we examined in the last chapter. His account shows that, like the Indigenous understanding of place, for much of Western history ethics and meaning were encountered out in the cosmos, and that the discovery of the modern universe had the unintended consequence of killing the cosmos and leaving ethics without a foundation. Not only was the premodern Western cosmos alive and organic (as discussed in the next chapter), but it was viewed as so perfect that it was reverenced and loved. This *amor mundi*, love of the world, is a remarkable contrast to the modern world alienation and the technological domination of the world.

Brague is not saying that every person throughout Western history experienced the cosmos exactly in this way. He recognizes that there were diverse understandings of the world in the West, especially in popular understanding (medieval peasants, for example, had some wild ideas about the nature of the world). Nonetheless, he claims that there was a "standard vision of the world" that predominated among the educated and in the intellectual traditions of the West. This "standard vision of the world" combined the metaphysical articulation of the cosmos in Plato's late dialogue *Timaeus* with the Abrahamic faiths. The resulting model dominated

Western understanding for over a thousand years, until the rise of modern science and the discovery of the universe. Despite some inevitable variations and emphasis, "everyone had the same description of the world."[1] This was in large part because this understanding of the world was taken to be empirical. If you doubted it, you could go out and look for yourself. According to the "standard vision of the world," then, what was the structure of the cosmos?

2.1   THE METAPHYSICAL STRUCTURE OF THE COSMOS

According to the standard model, the Earth was at the center of the cosmos. This was not a random choice. When you look outside at the stars by night or at the sun and the clouds by day, they appear to move around the Earth. Now, modern science teaches us that the Earth is both moving rapidly through space and spinning while doing so, which is why it appears that everything in the skies is moving around it. This claim was known to ancient astronomers but viewed as controversial or doubtful because, if it were so, why doesn't everything on the Earth fly off it? Gravity, we now say. But gravity wasn't theorized until Newton. In fact, for some time after Copernicus showed the Earth was not in the center until Newton, scientists and philosophers posited the existence of an "aether" that surrounded the earth and prevented everything from flying off it.

It is important to note that modern science and modern physics reveal a world that is in many ways counter-intuitive and defies everyday experience (a bowling ball and a feather falling at the same speed in a vacuum is the classic example). For the ancients looking around at their world, it was obvious that the Earth was stationary and that everything else rotated around it. Just look!

When they looked at the skies above, they noticed that the stars moved in fixed patterns across the sky in an arc. In fact, if you can escape the light pollution to see the sky clearly at night, it looks like the entire sky is fixed to a sphere that is rotating around the Earth, much like projections in a planetarium. Some objects in the night sky, like the moon, also move in arcs, but not in the same arcs as the rest of the sky. From this fact it is reasonable to conclude that there are multiple spheres nestled inside each other. Altogether, then, the cosmos is like an onion, with the Earth at the center and with multiple spheres surrounding and rotating around the Earth.

The stars above move in such regular patterns that sailors could navigate by the stars at night. This constancy in the heavens contrasts with what happens on the Earth around us. Here we do not see seemingly eternal patterns, but perpetual change: humans age, plants and animals die, rivers dry up, rain comes and goes, mountains slowly but surely erode. Nothing stays the same. Human experience and embodiment itself are driven by changing moods, fluctuating hunger and sexual desire, the hubbub and perpetual movement of daily life, crowds, opinions, changing one's mind, disruptions—in short, the world around us, in contrast to the stars above us, seems to be perpetually changing and shifting. Based on these obvious differences, Plato concludes that everything above the sphere of the moon was unchanging, regular, and eternal, while everything below the sphere of the moon was changing and shifting. The sphere of the moon, then, divides the realm of being above from the realm of becoming below the moon.

The word "cosmos" in Greek means "order." We can now see why. The cosmos above is literally a regular, predictable order. For Plato, this has radical implications in terms of how we understand ethics.

2.2 ETHICS AND HUMAN NATURE IN THE TIMAEAN COSMOS

Up until this point, the account of the cosmos is empirical. It is based on what we see when we look at the world around us. But for Plato, the order that is the cosmos has moral implications.

Plato is famously wary of the desires and emotions of the physical body. Hunger, sexual desire, and emotions can make us "irrational" and are the source of much of the chaos of human life. For Plato, a better society and a better life are achieved by controlling desire and emotions. The Timaean Cosmos builds this problem into the cosmos itself (or, depending on what you think Plato is doing, finds the solution in the cosmos itself). The realm of being above the moon is a realm of perfect order. Humans live below the moon in the realm of becoming. As odd as it sounds to modern ears, if we want to improve our personal lives and our communities, we must look to and imitate the stars in the realm of being above us. To imitate the stars means to seek to live an ordered life, which, among other things, involves controlling our emotions and desires and seeking to achieve heavenly equanimity.

The realm of being is not just there, however. For Christians, Jews, and Muslims it was created and put there by a benevolent God. For all the potential chaos and pain of life on Earth, we are always surrounded by a realm of pure goodness—and as such, "evil is the exception."[2] When we understand the moral valences of the Timaean Cosmos, we find ourselves in a place very different from the modern universe, which is incomprehensible, vast, and devoid of morality. The Timaean Cosmos is entirely visible, comprehensible, and morality is literally written above us across the skies. This world is, Brague claims, "a happy world."[3] It is very much our home.

As if this were not enough, the cosmos calls to us, not only because it is attractive aesthetically and morally, but because we have an affinity with it. We humans are a microcosm of the cosmos.[4] We have a rational soul inside our physical body—an inverted form of the cosmos in which the imperfect realm surrounds the rational. Even our physical structure mirrors the cosmos in important ways. Our "erect posture" points us toward the sky.[5] Medieval thinkers pointed out patterns in the human body:

> Thus in miniatures in which a man is shown nude, his arms extended to form a cross, inscribed in a square, his head surrounded by a circle, or simply inscribed within a circle—two images that a familiar drawing by Leonardo da Vinci ingeniously attempts to combine. The human form, presented as a *chi* (X), imitates not only the Cross of Christ, but the intersection of the circles of the soul which, according to the Timaeus, defines the world.[6]

It is almost as if the cosmos has left us hints to find the truth: "man [*sic*] contains within himself what he needs to know the entire universe."[7] But the cosmos is not content with mere hints; it is active in calling to us: "Through influences, the world calls on man, as if magnetically, to allow himself to be infused by it."[8] Of course, from the perspective of the Abrahamic faiths, this testifies to the goodness of God.

2.3 CONTEMPLATE THE COSMOS

So how do humans tap into or connect with the cosmos? Through contemplation. In contemporary life, we now tend to discourage contemplation. We reward and encourage productive thinking, thinking that solves problems and gets results. There are still some moments in modern life when we might contemplate; for example, while visiting a beautiful national park, watching a thought-provoking film, or walking through a museum. A compelling piece of art or a beautiful landscape can speak to us. It can impose itself on us, shock us, stop us in our tracks, challenge us, and make us think. Contemplation opens something up for us, immersing us in a landscape or sweeping us up in a story.

For those living in the Timaean Cosmos, contemplation was the primary means of aligning oneself with and being influenced by it. Brague points out that for the ancient thinkers Seneca and Plotinus, "to be concerned with the objects of contemplation" was not unproductive, but rather, as strange as this might sound to us now, "to be actively involved in the highest form of politics."[9] Contemplating the cosmos is an act of communion. It makes us better and we could then potentially make others better. "The dignity of contemplation and the dignity of the world are mutually reinforced: it is because contemplation is the loftiest activity that it has bearing on the world; reciprocally, it is the supreme dignity of the world that endows contemplation with all its worth."[10]

It is not to say that contemplation was enough. Self-discipline and a host of other practices would have been required depending on the particular traditions. But contemplation was such a central practice until modernity that the twentieth-century German philosopher Hannah Arendt describes the entire period in the West between Plato and the rise of modernity as being oriented by the *vita contemplative*.[11]

2.4 THE DISCOVERY OF THE UNIVERSE AND THE DEATH OF THE COSMOS
If the cosmos was indeed such a wonderful place, what happened to it and how has it been so thoroughly forgotten?

The death of the cosmos was an accident. No one set out to kill it. Rather, modern science revealed that the universe is not as Plato described. Careful observation of the stars showed problems: spots on the sun; strange retrograde movements from Mercury; comets beyond the sphere of the moon moved out of sync with the rest of the stars. With time, it was shown that the Earth is not stationary and instead is flying through space. We don't fall off due to gravity. While the moon does orbit the Earth, it doesn't separate two distinct realms, and it turns out the supposed realm of being actually is vast, expanding, and ultimately incomprehensible. Brague points out that the word "universe" means something like "the one big thing" or "all the stuff." The connotation of order implied by the cosmos is gone, replaced by something that some might find fascinating but is no longer a home. The twentieth-century German philosopher Hans Jonas's description of the situation is worth quoting at length:

> Gone is the cosmos with whose immanent *logos* my own can feel kinship, gone the order of the whole in which man has his place. That place appears now as a sheer and brute accident. 'I am frightened and amazed,' continues [the French philosopher] Pascal, 'at finding myself here rather than there; for there is no reason whatever why here rather than there, why now rather than then.' There had always been a reason for the 'here,' so long as the cosmos had been regarded as man's [sic] natural home, that is, so long as the world had been understood as 'cosmos.' But Pascal speaks of 'this remote corner of nature' in which man should 'regard himself as lost,' of 'the little prison-cell in which he finds himself lodged, I mean the (visible) universe.' The utter

contingency of our existence in the scheme deprives that scheme of any human sense as a possible frame of reference for understanding of ourselves.

But there is more to this situation than the mere mood of homelessness, forlornness, and dread. The indifference of nature also means that nature has no reference to ends. With the ejection of teleology from the system of natural causes, nature, itself purposeless, ceased to provide any sanction to possible human purposes. A universe without an intrinsic hierarchy of being, as the Copernican universe is, leaves values ontologically unsupported, and the self is thrown back entirely upon itself in its quest for meaning and value. Meaning is no longer found but is 'conferred.' Values are no longer beheld in the vision of objective reality, but are posited as feats of valuation.[12]

When the cosmos is replaced by the universe, humanity not only loses a home, but it also loses its visible source of meaning, purpose, and ethics. True, one could see these as originating or rooted in the God that created the cosmos; but when the cosmos died, traditional belief in God was also threatened for many. If God's beautiful cosmos was gone, where was God?

Now, to be clear, it is not as if the discovery of the universe and the death of the cosmos happened instantaneously, or that the implications were immediately clear. In fact, the German philosopher Nietzsche wrote in the late 1800s that the implications of these changes were still not clear to many people:

> What were we doing when we unchained this earth from the sun? Whither is it moving now? Whither are we moving? Away from all suns? Are we not plunging continually? Backward, sideward, forward, in all directions? Is there still any up or down? Are we not straying as through an infinite nothing? Do we not feel the breath of empty space? Has it not become colder? Is not night continually closing in on us?[13]

For Pascal and Nietzsche (and we could also add Deloria and Wildcat), the death of the cosmos is a tragic and traumatic event with radical implications for human (and nonhuman) existence. But, the fact of the matter is, most people now are not bothered by this. More to the point, most people don't even know this happened. The cosmos and what it meant for humans has been largely forgotten in the West. But how could something so important be forgotten? This is a complicated question, but Brague has a worrying explanation.

2.5 A NEW ETHICS FOR A NEW UNIVERSE

The modern universe has a completely different metaphysical makeup than the cosmos. While the cosmos was the "reign of the good," the universe ostensibly is neither good nor bad. It just is. But in practice "modern nature, present above all in biological facts, appears to be the kingdom of evil."[14] This is because modern nature does not provide adequately for human needs. Not only is it lacking, but it can also be dangerous. "Since the good is not in nature, it is thus necessary to introduce it into nature. And by force, by taking nature against the grain."[15] Humans must fix nature and make it less dangerous and more useful for humankind. Technology is what enables humans to tame nature: "Modern technology defines itself through an undertaking of domination, through a plan to become, according to the famous epigram of [the French philosopher] Descartes, the 'master and possessor of nature'."[16]

The new universe, which is made up of physical matter and often articulated in early modernity as being like a machine (more on this in the next chapter), practically begs for human intervention. Brague claims that since modern technology allows us to better the human condition by battling and overcoming nature, it functions as a moral practice. Technology in modernity, then, is a "form of morality, and perhaps even true morality."[17] Technology spreads good and ameliorates the human condition by understanding and controlling nature.

In the modern universe, there is no more reason to contemplate the stars. Instead of wasting our time contemplating the heavens, look to humankind—what we need is to make the world intelligible through science and solve its problematic inadequacies through technology. In a very real sense, Brague claims, humans are all that really matters in modernity. The world is humanized.

Thus, with this new moral orientation toward the world (understand, control, improve), the old concerns about the death of the cosmos, like the cosmos itself, have largely faded away. I teach this text by Brague regularly and before we read anything from it, I have my classes do a word association exercise. I ask them to write down what they think of when I say the word "cosmos." What they come up with are words that we would associate with the modern universe: "vast," "empty," "space," "planets," "cold," "incomprehensible," "constellations." Occasionally I get "meaningless," "scary," and "aliens." Only once have I ever had a student write "home." I've never had students say "order," "perfection," "morality," or "ethics." The cosmos really is mostly forgotten in popular memory.

The fact of the matter is that science and technology have indeed allowed us to change much of the world in ways that are extending human life and making it more comfortable for us. It is not surprising that people are excited about technology and that much of our education and jobs are tied up in this moral task of creating new technologies and making life better.

From an environmental perspective, the death of the cosmos and the rise of technology as morality is a disaster. It is especially disturbing how modern technology and, if Brague is right, modern morality, are defined over and against nature. For the world to be reshaped and humanized, nature must be dominated and possessed. We turn to this topic in the next chapter.

2.6 QUESTIONS FOR DISCUSSION

1. What is the structure of the "standard model" of the cosmos? What is the moral significance of this structure?
2. Why was contemplation so important in the cosmos? What has replaced it now?
3. What happened to the cosmos? How is it different from the modern universe?
4. Why does Brague think technology is "perhaps even true morality" in the modern universe? Do you think this is dangerous? Why?

2.7 FURTHER READING

In addition to Brague's *The Wisdom of the World: The Experience of the Universe in Western Thought*, another prominent discussion of the shift from the cosmos to the universe is Alexandre Koyre's classic *From the Closed World to the Infinite Universe*. Hans Jonas explores how our understanding of life and death has shifted in *The Phenomenon of Life: Toward a Philosophical Biology*. David Abram has discussed how these changes affect how we perceive the world in *The Spell of the Sensuous*.

Notes

1 Brague, Rémi. *The Wisdom of the World: The Experience of the Universe in Western Thought* (Chicago: University of Chicago Press, 2003).
2 Ibid., 108.
3 Ibid., 106.
4 Ibid., 98.
5 Ibid., 99.
6 Ibid., 94.
7 Ibid., 95.
8 Ibid., 98.

9 Brague, 124.
10 Ibid., 122.
11 Arendt, Hannah. *The Human Condition* (Chicago: University of Chicago Press, 1998).
12 Jonas, Hans. *The Phenomenon of Life: Toward a Philosophical Biology* (Evanston, IL: Northwestern University Press, 2001), 214–15.
13 Ibid.
14 Brague, 209.
15 Ibid.
16 Ibid.
17 Ibid., 210.

3

THE DEATH OF NATURE

This chapter builds on the last two by looking at Carolyn Merchant's *The Death of Nature: Women, Ecology and the Scientific Revolution*. Merchant will echo the concerns of Deloria and Wildcat about the predatory and abusive aspects of modern science and technology and affirm the radical implications of the death of the cosmos and nature. What she adds to these accounts is a keen focus on the role of gender in these dynamics.

Her argument is straightforward and powerful. She claims that the scientific revolution led to a shift from an organic, animistic cosmos to a dead, mechanical universe. This radical change in understanding the metaphysics of the world also marks fundamental changes in the ethical relationships between humans and the world around them. These relationships were guided by pivotal gendered metaphors: mother earth on the one hand and disordered nature (embodied in the witch) on the other. Her account alerts us to a disturbing gendered violence in modernity.

3.1 THE WORLD AS ORGANISM

Feminists have argued that a bizarre masculine hyper-individualism in early modern political thinkers has become widespread in modern Western self-understanding and encoded in modern politics and laws.[1] Originally this manifested not only in literary narratives such as *Robinson Crusoe* (a rugged person fighting for survival alone on an island) but also in narratives invoked by early modern thinkers that begin with the lone individual, his work, his property, and his rights, and the question of how these lone individuals come together to form a society. Condillac's theory of language starts with two strangers talking in a desert. Adam Smith imagines two individuals bartering their goods. René Descartes meditates in his room with no one around (and concludes that the one thing he can be sure of is that he exists and thinks; he can't be sure if anyone else exists). Thomas Hobbes begins his famous political theory by asking us to "look at men as if they had just emerged from the earth like mushrooms and grown up without any obligation to each other."[2] These accounts are all very odd in that they start with one or two autonomous individuals. No mothers, no children, no elderly, no community, no obligations.

This modern individualistic atomism stands in remarkable contrast to premodern understanding. According to Merchant,

> The world we have lost was organic. From the obscure origins of our species, human beings have lived in daily, immediate organic relation with the natural order for their sustenance. In 1500, the daily inter-action with nature was still structured for most Europeans, as it was for other peoples, by close-knit, cooperative, organic communities.[3]

Here Merchant uses the word "organic," which has connotations of "natural" but should also be understood as connected with "organ" and "organism." When Merchant claims the world we have lost was organic, she means that the world was viewed as an interconnected organism. This kind of interconnection is what is stressed by ecology—"that everything is connected to everything else...All parts are dependent on one another and mutually affect each other and the whole."[4] As we saw in the last chapter, humans are connected to the cosmos and nature around us in an "organic unity." Merchant quotes Giambattista della Porta (1535–1615): "The whole world is knit and bound within itself: for the world is a living creature, everywhere both male and female, and the parts of it do couple together...by reason of their mutual love." Because of this indelible interpenetration "when one part suffers the rest also suffers with it."[5]

The same was held to be true not only of the whole cosmos, but of human society. Different parts of society were necessary for the functioning of all, from the king or prince at the top to the priests, warriors, and peasants. "The medieval theory of society thus stresses the whole before the parts, while emphasizing the inherent values of each particular part."[6]

3.2 NATURE AS FEMALE

So far, this squares with what Brague argued. But Merchant also argues that gender is important to understanding these dynamics: "Central to the organic theory was the identification of nature, especially the earth, with a nurturing mother: a kindly beneficent female who provided for the needs for mankind in an ordered, planned universe."[7] This metaphor of nature as our mother is deeply significant and fundamentally shaped how humans understood and interacted with the natural world:

> The image of the earth as a living organism and nurturing mother had served as a cultural constraint restricting the actions of human beings. One does not readily slay a mother, dip into her entrails for gold or mutilate her body, although commercial mining would soon require that. As long as the earth was considered to be alive and sensitive, it could be considered a breach of human ethical behavior to carry out destructive acts against it. For most traditional cultures, minerals and metals ripened in the uterus of the Earth Mother, mines were compared to her vagina, and metallurgy was the human hastening of the birth of the living meal in the artificial womb of the furnace—an abortion of the metal's natural growth cycle before its time.[8]

If the earth is understood to be a mother, then mining is akin to rape. This view was voiced in Edmund Spenser's *Faerie Queene* and John Milton's *Paradise Lost*, where mining is portrayed by Milton as being driven by avarice and rapacious lust:

> Men also, and by his suggestion taught,
> Ransack'd the Center, and with impious hands
> Rifl'd the bowels of their mother Earth
> For Treasures better hid. Soon has his crew
> Op'nd into the Hill a spacious wound
> And dig'd out ribs of Gold.[9]

When the Earth is understood to be our mother, humankind needs to relate to her with caution, care, respect, and love. The things that she gives to us, her children, are gifts and they need to be received with gratitude and thanksgiving. They should not be hoarded from her other children but should be shared. Furthermore, we need to give back to Mother Earth and protect her from those who would attack her.

Like the Native American understanding of power and place according to Deloria and Wildcat and the premodern understanding of the cosmos according to Brague, it is easy to understand intellectually the idea that the Earth is our Mother, but it is difficult to practically grasp how radically this would shape everyday understanding and action. To do so would likely require a sensitive anthropological approach because it is so alien from how we currently understand the world and relate to it. This shift away from Mother Earth is the focus of the rest of Merchant's argument.

3.3 NATURE AS DISORDER

Merchant claims that the traditional understanding of the Earth as our Mother constrained commercial activity and circumscribed the scope of human intervention on and into the Earth. "But another opposing image of nature as female was also prevalent: wild and uncontrollable nature that could render violence, storms, droughts, and general chaos." Here a different gendered metaphor is invoked, one of nature as a wild, uncontrollable woman. Merchant quotes the Italian thinker Machiavelli (1469–1527):

> Fortune is the ruler of half our actions...I would compare her to an impetuous river that when turbulent, inundates the plains, casts down trees and buildings, removes earth from this side and places it on the other; everyone flees before it and everything yields to its fury without being able to oppose it; and yet though it is of such a kind, still when it is quiet, men can make provision against it by dikes and banks, so that when it rises it will either go down a canal or its rush will not be so wild and dangerous. So it is with fortune, which shows her power where no measures have been taken to resist her, and directs her fury where she knows that no dikes or barriers have been made to hold her.[10]

Instead of respecting nature, Machiavelli argues that she must be subdued through physical violence:

> For fortune is a woman and it is necessary if you wish to master her, to conquer her by force; and it can be seen that she lets herself be overcome by the bold rather than by those who proceed coldly, and therefore like a woman, she is always a friend to the young because they are less cautious, fiercer, and master her with greater audacity.[11]

Here we see language akin to rape being invoked not to *condemn* certain human activities, but to *promote* them: "the new images of master and domination function as cultural sanctions for the denudation of nature."[12] Merchant points out how the language in early modern science (and still today) is full of metaphors of "revealing" and "discovering" the secrets of nature. Mother is no longer being protected, but unclothed, her secrets revealed to the gaze of the men of science.

Thus, we have on the one hand language that is, at times, overtly sexualized. On the other hand (and, of course, at times intertwined with sexualized language), there is language that is violent and aimed at nature as a chaotic and unruly force. Merchant points out that there is a parallel here between the witch and nature. The witch is the uncontrollable wild woman of the woods. She is scary, dangerous, unpredictable, and must be hunted down and destroyed. For Merchant, the coincidence of the rise of modernity and witch hunts is not an accident, but an expression of a fundamental violence on the part of modernity. This violence was not only justified in the name of overcoming the wild, but also through another key metaphor: the machine and the mechanical order.

3.4 THE MECHANICAL ORDER

The sexualized and violent language aimed at witches and their disorderly nature is deeply disturbing. A second less disturbing metaphor was also invoked to justify scientific intervention into nature: nature as a machine.

If nature is a woman, indeed our mother, then we need to respect her and not rapaciously steal from her. But if nature is a machine, our interventions are not only not rapacious but morally justified. A broken machine must be fixed. Even a well-functioning machine could perhaps run even better if we make appropriate changes.

> The brilliant achievement of mechanism as a world view was its reordering of reality around two fundamental constituents of human experience—order and power. Order was attained through an emphasis on the motion of indivisible parts subject to mathematical laws and the rejection of unpredictable animistic sources of change. Power was achieved through immediate active intervention in a secularized world.[13]

Unlike an organic world, the mechanical world begged for intervention. For Merchant, the modern world is built on the ideas of "mechanism and the domination and mastery of nature."[14] Science is the tool that allows humans to understand the world, reveal her/its secrets, and then potentially use technology to control her/it. Over time, the scientific method has been increasingly described as a neutral method that produces "objective, value-free, and context-free knowledge of the external world."[15] The sexualized and violent language has been toned down and the language of neutrality and authority have become more common. To present science in this fashion strips it of its own history and the kinds of metaphors that have surrounded and justified scientific activities for the last 400 years. Of course, historians of science and philosophers of science have long complained that this innocuous understanding of science is not only inaccurate, but propagandistic: it is actively shielding science and technology from scrutiny. This claim would be echoed by Vinc Deloria Jr., who consistently warned of the ways in which science has been and continues to be marshaled in colonial fashion against Native Americans. Merchant shows that the language of "revealing" and "discovering" retains a residue of the violence and sexualization of nature.

3.5 THE DEATH OF NATURE

Whether modern science meant to or not, Merchant claims it has played a key role in the death of nature. Both Merchant and Brague would agree with Hans Jonas that "[o]ur thinking today is under the ontological dominance of death."[16] This remarkable phrase is his way of marking the difference between the panpsychism of premodernity and the "panmechanism" of modernity. When all is machine, life itself becomes a phenomenon that is difficult to explain: "To take life as a problem is here to acknowledge its strangeness in the mechanical world which is *the* world."[17]

Jonas claims that in many premodern cultures, life was everywhere. What was difficult to explain was death. But as modernity increasingly saw the world as a machine, life became a question:

> Death is the natural thing, life the problem. From the physical science there spread over the conception of all existence an ontology whose model entity is pure matter, stripped of all features of life... The tremendously enlarged universe of modern cosmology is conceived as a field of inanimate masses and forces which operate according to the laws of inertia and of quantitative distribution in space. This denuded substratum of all reality could only be arrived at through a progressive expurgation of vital features from the physical record and through strict abstention from projecting into its image our felt aliveness.[18]

For Jonas, early modern thought adopted the mechanical worldview with the hopes that it would result in not only a better understanding of the world but control over it. Critically, however, the dead corpse universe obscures fundamental aspects of the cosmos even as it illuminates the universe: "waiving the intelligibility of life—the price which modern knowledge was willing to pay for its title to the greater part of reality—renders the world unintelligible as well. And the reduction of teleological to mechanical causality, great as its advantages are for analytic description, has gained nothing in the matter of comprehending the nexus itself: the one is no less mysterious than the other."[19] What Jonas means by this is that while the shift to a mechanical understanding does give us control over the world, it makes it harder to understand an obvious reality: the life we see all around us! Not only is the fundamental reality of life obscured, but the kinds of ethical questions that have traditionally surrounded life—how to respect it, how to interact with it, how to foster it—also become muddled and confused. The cosmos is dead, nature is dead, what does this mean?

This is the conundrum announced in a famous aphorism by Friedrich Nietzsche in a story entitled "The Madman." In this story, a person with a severely disordered state of mind appears in the marketplace in the middle of the day with a lit lamp and yells to everyone around that God is dead. Not just that God is dead, but that we have killed God. This presents a conundrum Nietzsche thought Western society had brought on itself while not yet realizing it: we have radically altered the world in modernity but are so excited by these changes that we don't see what we have lost. When Nietzsche's character announces the death of God, those who no longer believe in God mock the character. They do not yet realize what they have done.

Similarly, Deloria, Wildcat, Brague, and Merchant are telling us that Western modernity has killed the cosmos and killed our own Mother Nature, and yet it is not clear that most people in modernity recognize what has happened. Sadly, in the midst of our consumer abundance, many believe that life goes on better than ever before. On the contrary, the thinkers we are examining claim that life does not go on and that Western arrogance threatens not only humanity but the Earth and all the nonhuman peoples on it.

3.6 PROGRESS?

It is easy to be blinded by the successes of modernity and not see its destructive and colonial aspects. Proponents and defenders of modernity tend to stress that everything is better than it was before: GDP is higher, life expectancy is higher, there is less violence, less disease, and more order.

Even if we accept these gains, the current global climate crisis shows there are great dangers involved. Arguably the *human* condition is better (and it should be stressed that this is arguable—human life in the cosmos has its own merits), but the *nonhuman* condition is not. The very condition of human existence, the Earth, is being radically altered by human action. This is leading to human-caused mass extinction. From an Indigenous perspective, the progress of modernity seems to coincide with genocide against the nonhuman peoples of the Earth and the cultural destruction of non-modern humanity. Indeed, when Osage chief Big Soldier observed Western "progress" in 1820, he claimed:

> I see and admire your manner of living, your good warm houses, your extensive fields of corn, your gardens, your cows, oxen, workhouses, wagons, and a thousand machines that I know not the use of. I see that you are able to clothe yourselves, even from weeds and grass. In short, you even do almost what you choose. You are surrounded by slaves. Everything about you is in chains, and you are slaves yourselves. I fear if I should exchange my pursuits for yours, I too should become a slave.[20]

Big Soldier recognizes the material gains of Western life but rejects them as deeply unethical and critically flawed. A skeptical advocate of modernity that rejects the Native American metaphysics of power and place will say that the claim of "slavery" does not hold for mere things. The modern world is not full of life and thus cannot be enslaved. But Big Solider is not just making a claim about the unethical treatment of nonhuman peoples. He says, "you are slaves yourselves." This could be understood in different ways. Big Soldier could be saying that humans are also treated poorly in modernity; this is a common claim that has repeatedly been raised during and since the Romantic movement (early 1800s). Or he could be claiming that humans are caught up in the obsession with the accumulation of money and property or caught up and unfree in the machinery of modernity. Whatever he means exactly, the challenge here is to the supposed superiority of modernity. Big Soldier is saying that it is not a good life.

The purpose of these first three chapters is not to claim that everyone must recover or adopt an Indigenous or premodern Western metaphysics (in any case, one can't just take off and put on a worldview like clothing), but primarily to challenge the naïve supposed superiority of modern Western thought and practice. Western practices are driving global climate change, mass extinction, and environmental disaster. As we will see in the next sections, environmental theories and movements have challenged the tendency in Western practices to seek technological Band-Aids to modern environmental destruction. Environmental philosophers have claimed we need more radical changes. Before turning to these issues, however, we should examine one more argument about premodern metaphysics, an argument that has shaped Western modernity.

3.7 QUESTIONS FOR DISCUSSION

1. Even today, we sometimes hear the Earth referred to as "Mother Earth." For Merchant, what is the significance of this?
2. Some feminists have pointed out that men are often defined over and against nature. To be a man is to fight and win against nature. Do you think this kind of domination still plays a role in "masculine" identity?
3. Is it correct to say that nature is often treated like a machine? What example have you seen of this?

3.8 FURTHER READING

Merchant's *The Death of Nature: Women, Ecology and the Scientific Revolution* is often considered an early and classic example of ecofeminism. Val Plumwood's *Feminism and the Master of Nature* clearly pays homage to Merchant. For more discussion of ecofeminism, see Chapter 7. As mentioned in the last chapter, the question of life and death in nature is explored in Hans Jonas's *The Phenomenon of Life: Toward a Philosophical Biology.*

Notes

1 Kittay, Eva Feder. *Love's Labor: Essays on Women, Equality and Dependency* (New York: Routledge, 1999).
2 Hobbes, Thomas. *Hobbes: On the Citizen* (New York: Cambridge University Press, 1998), 102.
3 Merchant, Carolyn. *The Death of Nature: Women, Ecology and the Scientific Revolution* (New York: Harper and Row, 1990), 1.
4 Ibid., 99.
5 Ibid., 104.
6 Ibid., 70.
7 Ibid., 2.
8 Ibid., 3–4.
9 Ibid., 39.
10 Ibid., 130.
11 Ibid.
12 Ibid., 2.

13 Ibid., 216.
14 Ibid., 2.
15 Ibid., 290.
16 Jonas, Hans. *The Phenomenon of Life: Toward a Philosophical Biology* (Evanston, IL: Northwestern University Press, 2001), 12.
17 Ibid., 11.
18 Ibid., 9–10.
19 Ibid., 25.
20 Deloria, Jr., Vine. *Spirit and Reason: The Vine Deloria, Jr., Reader* (Golden, CO: Fulcrum, 1999), 4.

4

RELIGION AND THE ENVIRONMENT

All the books by the authors discussed in the first three chapters have argued from different perspectives that the contemporary environmental crisis is related to the metaphysics of modernity. This is to say, there is something about how modern thought and practice understand the nature of the world and ourselves (humankind) that is leading to both an alienation from the world and a willingness to exploit that world. Critically, these assumptions about the nature of the world are almost always taken for granted. Like a fish swimming in water, modern Western peoples (and increasingly more modernizing non-Western peoples) now find this way of understanding and living in the world both normal and natural, even if, as Deloria and Wildcat argue, it is destructive. But if we compare the modern Western experience with non-Western or premodern Western experiences, we find very different ways of relating to the world. Deloria and Wildcat confront modern Western thought with Native American thought and experience. Brague, Merchant, and Jonas contrast modern Western assumptions with the premodern West. Seeing and understanding other traditions and ways of relating to the world has the potential to disrupt naturalized modern understandings and practices and hopefully make us stop and think about what we are doing.

This chapter seeks to add an additional argument to these claims and also head off some potential misunderstandings. These misunderstandings are centered on the supposed opposition between religion and science. The famous argument of Lynn White Jr. shows not only that modern science is rooted in premodern Christianity, but also (although this was not his intention) that the supposed opposition of religion and science is far too simplistic. Let us look at this supposed opposition before examining Lynn White Jr.'s argument itself.

4.1 SCIENCE VS. RELIGION

Despite the objections of historians and philosophers of science, science and religion are often treated as rivals. Religion is often associated with tradition and conservativism, while science is often associated with technological progress and change. At times, this opposition is fostered by the religious organizations or scientific groups themselves. Thus, we find at times fundamentalist-leaning religious groups that call for privileging religion over science—for example, as a test of faith, encouraging members to pray for help from God instead of visiting a doctor. We also find some advocates of science attacking religious beliefs as backward and dangerous. Often claims that religion and science are enemies are politicized. Thus, we find far-right politicians claiming that freedom of religion is under attack from "secular progressives" on the one hand, and on the other, left-leaning advocates lamenting how religious zealotry is leading to certain forms of science denial (rejection of climate science, opposition to masks during a pandemic, etc.).

There is a related opposition in philosophy. This is the opposition between epistemology and metaphysics. Recall that epistemology concerns knowledge and how we know. Science is a method of knowing. Revelation is a method of knowing for many religious people. Metaphysics concerns the nature of reality or the nature of a particular thing in question. A chair, the number two, and love are very different things. Their being or ontology is different. A chair is a physical object made of matter. The number two is an idea. Love is a complicated thing depending on what we mean by 'love'. Either way, these have distinct ontological natures.

In modern philosophy, metaphysics is often associated with unscientific speculation. This is because, it has been argued, modern philosophy was responding to the often religiously based arguments of medieval philosophers that were often functioning within a theological framework of Catholicism.[1] Medieval philosophers debated many things, but often these were connected to religious questions concerning the nature and existence of God or delimited by theological constraints. From a modern perspective, some of these debates seem very strange and rooted in biblical scripture rather than "reality." Modern philosophy sought to (or at least with time has articulated itself as seeking to) find a method that would cut through the metaphysical speculations and fluff of much of medieval philosophy. That is to say, modern philosophy was concerned with seeking proper methods for knowing. Once the right ways of knowing could be established, it was hoped, the proper method could help resolve these convoluted debates. Later an approach called positivism would even insist that many of these speculative or "metaphysical" debates would disappear because there was no way of resolving them satisfactorily. The account I am offering here is of course simplistic, but it gives an indication of how modern philosophy came to label and oppose speculative issues about the nature and existence of God or angels or virtues, etc. as useless "metaphysics" and oppose this with the quest for effective epistemological methods that could deliver well-founded "truth."

While metaphysics and epistemology do not map onto religion and science perfectly, there are parallels. Science is an epistemological method that has become widely accepted as a successful way of understanding the nature of (physical) reality. Religion, like the characterization of metaphysics as wild speculation, is left cut off from truth and left in the realm of "belief."

The last three chapters might give the impression that Western modernity is fundamentally opposed to premodern and non-modern metaphysics and religion. Indeed, the very term "modern" emphasizes newness and a break from the past. So indeed, at times, science and religion seem to be cast as antagonists: many modern thinkers have claimed to be focused on epistemological questions of how to know correctly about the world first and hoped that establishing a proper, agreed-upon method would resolve conflicts about the nature of reality. In a certain sense, modern thinkers said we should hold off on metaphysical and religious questions until we had a method to find out the truth about them. But, as we saw with Deloria and Wildcat, the most successful method of knowing in modernity, science, can only tell us about the physical universe. Questions of spirituality, meaning, and ethics fall beyond science's purview. Unfortunately, sometimes the success of science at describing the physical universe is mistaken to mean that the physical universe is all there is and that spirituality, meaning, and ethics are mere values and narratives that are in our heads or our hearts. Ironically, this sneaks in a metaphysical worldview that reality is only what is physical, and that spirituality, meaning, and ethics are "subjective."

According to Deloria and Wildcat, one of the colonial effects of this privileging of modern science (and the ironic smuggling in of a certain metaphysical view of the world) has been the dismissal of non-modern ontologies or metaphysical understandings of the world as speculative and "useless." Just as modern philosophy sought to distance itself from medieval metaphysical debates, it now dismisses Native American experience and understanding as "metaphysical" and unscientific. Deloria is quite aggressive about preserving the distinction between religion and science and presents modern science as the colonial aggressor against Native American religious practices.

So, depending on what we mean by "religion" and "science," some thinkers would say there is indeed an antagonism between the two. But, at the same time, many historians and philosophers of science would stress that narratives about science vs. religion are often too simplistic, especially if we believe there is a hard break between them with the rise of modernity, as if there were modern science on the one hand and ancient or premodern speculative metaphysics on the other. Indeed, many if not all early modern philosophers were religious, and many, like the German philosopher Leibniz, saw modern science as something that would aid religion.[2] Thus there are two objections to the narrative that science and religion are opposed. The first is that we don't find an immediate, radical break between them with the rise of modernity, but initially continuity. The second is that the philosophical self-articulation of modernity as "scientific" and therefore free from metaphysics is completely wrong, and that despite attempting to distance itself from metaphysics it is actually importing certain metaphysical views.

It is the first claim, that there is actually continuity between Western "scientific" modernity and Western "metaphysical" premodernity, that Lynn White Jr.'s argument shows.[3] Let us turn to this argument now.

4.2 THE HISTORICAL ROOTS OF OUR ECOLOGICAL CRISIS

Lynn White Jr.'s "The Historical Roots of Our Ecological Crisis" was originally something of an environmental classic, was often anthologized, and stimulated many debates about his claims. Although with time it has become less well regarded by some and despite disagreements among critics, for our purposes White can stimulate thinking about the connections between religion and science. His basic argument is that exploitative Western metaphysics has its origin in (medieval) Christianity: "Since both our technological and our scientific movements got their start, acquired their character, and achieved their world dominance in the Middle Ages, it would seem that we cannot understand the nature of their present impact upon ecology without examining fundamental medieval assumptions and developments."[4] The implication, of course, is that there is no radical break with modernity, but a continuity of attitudes toward the natural world that originated in medieval Christianity and are carried on in modern science and technology. This means that, paradoxically, modern science has adopted a metaphysics while seeking to overcome metaphysics.

White believes that the "exploitative attitude" in Western thought is a result of the medieval Christian struggle against paganism:

In Antiquity every tree, every spring, every stream, every hill had its own genius loci, its guardian spirit. These spirits were accessible to men, but were very unlike men; centaurs, fauns, and mermaids show their ambivalence. Before one cut a tree, mined a mountain, or dammed a brook, it was important to placate the spirit in charge of that particular situation, and to keep it placated. By destroying pagan animism, Christianity made it possible to exploit nature in a mood of indifference to the feeling of natural objects.[5]

According to White, we begin to see the aggressive efforts to rule over nature in illustrated calendars around 830 CE. These images portray men "plowing, harvesting, chopping trees, butchering pigs. Man and nature are two things, and man is master."[6] While people in other traditions obviously also engaged in similar tasks, White sees these images as the beginning of a tradition that sought to disenchant nature, empty it of the spirits that were competitors with the Christian God, and then to control and rule it. White points out that the biblical narrative presents the Earth and the beings on it as inferior to humankind and God: "Man names all the animals, thus establishing his dominance over them. God planned all of this explicitly for man's benefit and rule; no item in the physical creation had any purpose save to serve man's purposes."[7] This introduced an ontological or metaphysical rift in the world. On the one side is the Earth and the animals on it, on the other is humankind and God. The latter are superior to the former and are called upon to rule over them: "Man shares, in great measure, God's transcendence of nature. Christianity, in absolute contrast to ancient paganism and Asia's religions (except, perhaps, Zoroastrianism), not only established a dualism of man and nature but also insisted that it is God's will that man exploit nature for his proper ends."[8] Dominating nature is a calling, not only to drive out the idolatrous spirits, but as a spiritual task of control of the self and world around us.

Based on this analysis, White makes the remarkable claim that "[e]specially in its Western form, Christianity is the most anthropocentric religion the world has seen."[9] This domineering anthropocentrism carries over into modernity and, ironically in light of the supposed antipathy of modernity to religion, animates it. The current ecological crisis, then, is driven by a metaphysics that empties the world and everything on it—except humans—of life and sanctity. There is an ethics that insists on dominating the world not only for our betterment, but also to affirm our supposed superiority. Modern science and technology are thus an extension of the religious mandate to dominate the world and improve the human condition.

White recognizes that Christianity is a complex tradition with multiple branches that are not all in agreement. He finishes his argument by pointing out that while he thinks this domineering attitude of control over the natural world is the standard version of Christianity that has been passed on to modern science and technology, there are other versions or articulations of Christianity that are not so domineering toward nature. Specifically, he points to St Francis of Assisi who seems to reject (if not wholesale then to some degree) the ontological division of the world into human and God on one side and everything else on the other. Francis preached to the birds and seemed to see the beings of the natural world as his brothers and sisters instead of as his inferiors. It is worth noting that Pope Francis has encouraged this version of Christianity in his encyclical *Laudato Si'*. It is not clear however that Pope Francis repudiates the fundamental ontological difference between humans and God on the one side and the natural world on the other. Pope Francis seems to preserve this difference while claiming that the human relationship to the natural world should be one not of domination but of stewardship and care.[10]

4.3 IMPLICATIONS

What are the implications of Lynn White Jr.'s argument? First, he believes that the current ecological crisis is clearly the result of modern science and technology and, by extension, of Christianity. He doubts that "disastrous ecological backlash can be avoided simply by applying to our problems more science and more technology. Our science and technology have grown out of Christian attitudes toward man's relation to nature which are almost universally held not only by Christians and neo-Christians but also by those who fondly regard themselves as post-Christians."[11]

There are two points here. First, modern science and technology have inherited from and continue to share with Christianity a metaphysical understanding of the world that ontologically divides humans from the rest of the natural world and affirms the superiority of humans. This in turn justifies and even provides an ethical imperative to exploit the natural world to better the human condition. This means that science, which is often presented merely as a powerfully effective method for understanding reality, is *not* just a mere method, but tacitly, and often unknown to itself, imports both a metaphysics and an ethics. This is exactly the claim made by Vine Deloria Jr. and Daniel Wildcat: science is not metaphysically and ethically innocent or pure, and yet this supposed purity is used to justify the colonial imposition of science and the crude dismissal of non-modern metaphysics!

Second, "More science and more technology are not going to get us out of the present ecologic crisis until we find a new religion, or rethink our old one."[12] Modern science and the Christian religion are *not* opposites on this account: they share a fundamental ontology and ethics. White's language here is quite ironic in light of the supposed opposition of religion and science, as he is essentially saying that modern science is a religion and that we need a new religion. Not only can we no longer pretend science is in opposition to religion, but, against the supposed rejection of religion for science, White seeks an alternative religion to the religion of science.

Speaking broadly, Lynn White Jr. is rejecting the facile division of the world into clearly delineable parts: science, religion, metaphysics, epistemology, ethics, etc. It turns out that these supposedly different fields cannot seem to be fully separated and that attempts to do so obscure how they are actually being influenced by what they have claimed to exclude. If one claims to be doing just science, there is a danger that those things that are ostensibly not science—like ethics, aesthetics, religion, and metaphysic—will actually play tacit roles in the science one is doing and/or in how it is received. Instead of pretending that what we are doing is purely one thing or another, a better approach is to recognize that such purity is impossible and to seek to track these different influences. This is not to claim that we could ever understand all the tensions going on. Rather, recognizing these tensions requires moving between multiple traditional academic disciplines. Fully exploring these dynamics is beyond the scope of this book.

To its credit, environmental philosophy has demonstrated a willingness to break disciplinary constraints. Perhaps the most obvious such violation is the willingness of many environmental writers to encourage spirituality and to include it in their writing. This blends religion, science, philosophy, art, metaphysics, epistemology, etc. in ways that are not standard and can be jarring to some readers. We will see this in the next chapter on deep ecology.

4.4 QUESTIONS FOR DISCUSSION

1. Religion and science are often portrayed as being at odds with each other in modern society. Why might this be a false assumption?

2. According to Lynn White Jr., what is the relationship of Christianity to science? What do they have to do with the current environmental crisis?

3. What might it look like to cut across traditional boundaries of academic disciplines (such as art and math, or biology and ethics)?

4.5 FURTHER READING

Lynn White Jr.'s "The Historical Roots of Our Ecological Crisis" and Pope Francis's encyclical *Laudato Si'* provide an interesting contrast. Much has been written from a Christian perspective on environmental stewardship. Laura Stone's *Religion and Environmentalism: Exploring the Issues* delves further into the topic.

Notes

1 Rorty, Richard. *Philosophy and the Mirror of Nature* (Princeton, NJ: Princeton University Press, 1981).
2 Neiman, Susan. *Evil in Modern Thought: An Alternative History of Philosophy* (Princeton, NJ: Princeton University Press, 2004).
3 He is just one voice of many that have argued this. See, for example, Kuhn, Thomas. *The Structure of Scientific Revolutions* (Chicago, IL: University of Chicago Press, 1996).
4 White, Jr., Lynn. "The Historical Roots of Our Ecological Crisis." *Science*, vol. 155, no. 3767 (10 March 1967), 1204–05.
5 Ibid., 1205.
6 Ibid.
7 Ibid.
8 Ibid.
9 Ibid.
10 Pope Francis. *Laudato Si': On Care for Our Common Home.* [Encyclical]. 2015.
11 White, Jr., 1205.
12 Ibid.

SECTION TWO

ENVIRONMENTAL THEORIES

The second section of this text presents four environmental theories. The third section presents three environmental movements. This will inevitably lead to questions. Why separate theories from movements? Deep ecology, which is presented here as a theory, can be also accurately described as a movement. The animal rights movement, which is presented in the next section, has adopted Peter Singer's philosophical work *Animal Liberation* as a foundational text and has strong theoretical roots.[1] Furthermore, environmental philosophy has long stressed the need for action, blurring the line between theory and activism.

Why not have one section on "theories and movements" instead of dividing these into two sections? I do so for pedagogical reasons: to preserve the tension. Environmental philosophy encourages us to get out and try and make a difference, but it also encourages us to articulate reasons for our actions and to think through what we are doing. Good environmental practice involves moving back and forth between action and thought.

Not only is there the potential concern about the separation of theories and movements, but also the problem of which theories get presented. Theories come and go, and some academics might aim for breadth and try and present as many theories as possible, while others might like to focus on the newest and current theories and debates. While there is value in both these approaches, this text focuses on some of the classic environmental theories because of their desperation, because they help establish fundamental themes of environmental philosophy, and because they made mistakes that we can learn from. Deep ecology challenges the ways environmental approaches can be superficial and inadequate. Ecocentrism alerts us to modern anthropocentrism and encourages us to think in terms of ecological holism. Ecofeminism requires we not only think about the situation of women in relation to environmental issues, but think intersectionally, recognizing how environmental issues are tied up with gender, race, and global issues. Bioregionalism encourages us to approach environmental issues locally and to get in touch with place.

These are not the only environmental theories, and they have their flaws, but they do a good job alerting us to the complexity of the environmental crisis and how it functions on multiple registers and must be addressed on multiple registers.

Note
1 Singer, Peter. *Animal Liberation* (New York: Harper, 2009).

5

DEEP ECOLOGY

Environmental philosophy has a particularly strong record of seeking to rethink the direction of modern society. This has involved a willingness to take an interdisciplinary approach and to learn from traditions that mainstream Western thought has marginalized. This is not without dangers, but it makes for an approach that can be very diverse and radical. This dynamic can be seen in one of the most prominent theories in environmental philosophy: deep ecology.

5.1 AGAINST THE DOMINANT PARADIGM

The basic worry in deep ecology is that many current environmental efforts are not adequate because they are not radical enough. The word "radical" here refers to the root, like a radish. Hence the claim is that many current environmental efforts do indeed do something, but they are not getting to the root of the problem. The name "deep ecology," then, is meant to draw attention to the difference between "shallow" environmental approaches that are superficial and inadequate and approaches that are more radical and fundamental.

According to Bill Devall, shallow approaches fail to challenge the "dominant paradigm" in modern society.[1] He means by this the "values, beliefs, habits, and norms" that are widely accepted now. These include a commitment to economic growth, that the main purpose of government is to enable the "production of commodities" to ensure the material wellbeing of citizens, and that technology can fix our problems. New is better than old, the future is better than the past, more is better than less, more commodities lead to a higher standard of living. Overall, the dominant paradigm privileges the economic and ties it directly to progress.

The economically driven dominant paradigm can recognize environmental problems, but it funnels them through this lens in such a way that it seeks technological solutions that don't fundamentally challenge economic growth. Devall calls environmental efforts that don't challenge the dominant paradigm "reformist environmentalism."[2] These approaches can include building parks, encouraging recycling, improving resource management, increasing awareness of environmental issues, developing ecofriendly practices and technologies, etc. These efforts are not bad; in fact, many of them have led to improvements. But the changes they suggest tend to be incremental and fail to radically challenge the status quo.

5.2 SHALLOW VS. DEEP ECOLOGY

Deep ecology claims the status quo is unsustainable and inadequate. According to Arne Naess, who coined the phrase "deep ecology," we see this when we compare shallow ecological approaches to deep ecological approaches.[3] To summarize Naess's six examples:

(1) Pollution. Shallow: approaches seek technological solutions, send polluting industries to the Global South, and use economic incentives to manage pollution. Deep: approaches examine how pollution affects entire ecosystems, not just humans, question how economic growth and technology are primary contributors to these issues, and critique how the Global North is externalizing pollution onto poorer countries.

(2) Resources. Shallow: approaches see the natural world as resources that can and should be used by humans. If humans use too many of them, market forces will increase their value and conserve them. Deep: approaches reject the idea that the natural world is comprised of resources and that human values are their only or primary measure. We need to examine and alter our productive and consumptive practices.

(3) Population. Shallow: human overpopulation is an issue for the Global South. Human welfare is privileged over ecosystem health. Deep: the rapid increase in human population is leading to environmental destruction worldwide.

(4) Cultural Diversity and Appropriate Technology. Shallow: Industrialized countries need to support the Global South as they modern-

ize and adapt modern practices. This will inevitably involve social and cultural changes. Deep: Western technologies may be part of the problem, not the solution. Modernization efforts are not only colonial but may alter traditional practices that may be or may have been more ecologically sustainable than Western practices. Modernization may be ecologically and culturally destructive.

(5) Land and Sea Ethics. Shallow: the natural world is divided into pieces that are the property of individuals. Wildlife, water, and land are resources that humans need to manage with the aid of technological innovations. Deep: Nature does not belong to humans and ecosystems are disrupted when they are divided and used according to the whim of human "owners." If we want to seriously protect the environment, we need to see it and treat it in terms of ecosystems with its own needs that may not fit with human purposes.

(6) Education and the Scientific Enterprise. Shallow: we need more experts, more technology, and more science. Deep: we need radical change to our economic system and the exploitative aspects of our technological and scientific practices. We need to shift to a more holistic approach that respects the biosphere more fundamentally.[4]

These are the examples that Naess articulated in 1986, before the scientific consensus of the danger of climate change. On that issue, we see very similar shallow approaches being taken: hope for technological solutions, use of economic incentives to encourage changes in behavior from companies and individuals, international commitments among nations regarding climate goals, and so forth. None of these approaches fundamentally challenge unsustainable economic practices or the modern faith in technological solutions. But what if these problems are caused by our metaphysics, economics, and technologies?

5.3 GOING DEEPER, LOOKING FOR ALTERNATIVES

The basic argument of deep ecology, then, is that modern industrialized countries are only superficially committed to the environment and that more serious efforts must be far more radical. This requires a fundamental rethinking and reworking of Western thought and practice. Challenging the assumptions that underlie and justify these practices is frustratingly difficult, as not only are they often taken for granted, but they are tied to modern self-understanding, meaning, purpose, and modern ethics. As we saw Rémi Brague argue in Chapter 2, technology is not just a neutral tool, but often functions as a moral imperative. Technology allows us to "fix" the world and make it better for humans. Not surprisingly, technology then has strong positive moral valences and can even function as a kind of modern faith. Shallow ecological approaches repeatedly seek technological solutions.

Deep ecology claims that there is something fundamentally flawed about this approach and is faced with the task of critically examining these assumptions and seeking alternatives. To do so, deep ecologists cast their nets far and wide. According to Devall, they turn to Eastern thought, Native American thought and practice, the minority of Western thinkers that criticize Western modernity, the scientific discipline of ecology, and art.[5] From Eastern and Native American thought and practice, they seek ways of understanding and acting in the world that are more balanced with the natural world. From critical Western thinkers, they seek to understand what has gone wrong. From the scientific discipline of ecology, they seek an approach that is holistic and address these issues by examining interrelations and systems instead of only parts. From art, they seek new ways of perceiving and experiencing the world.

This means that deep ecology tends to range over much broader terrain than typical academic work. This can be refreshing if one feels constrained by these limits, but it also comes with dangers. These dangers include potentially being superficial, appropriative, overly romantic, reductive, or colonialist. We will discuss these problems in more detail in other chapters.

This willingness to range far and wide also means that deep ecologists often include spiritual concerns in their writings and explore literary approaches. This doesn't mean that deep ecology is not interested in science—its very name points to ecology. If anything, deep ecology is concerned with radically changing our practices toward the natural world and each other, and this is not a matter of generating more scientific knowledge, but of changing how we live. We can see this with Naess's articulation of an eight-point "platform" of deep ecology.

5.4 PRINCIPLES OF DEEP ECOLOGY

Naess's platform of deep ecology is as follows:

(1) The wellbeing and flourishing of human and nonhuman life on Earth have value in themselves (synonyms: intrinsic value, inherent worth). These values are independent of the usefulness of the nonhuman world for human purposes.

(2) Richness and diversity of life forms contribute to the realization of these values and are also values in themselves.

(3) Humans have no right to reduce this richness and diversity except to satisfy vital needs.

(4) The flourishing of human life and cultures is compatible with a substantially smaller human population. The flourishing of nonhuman life *requires* a smaller human population.

(5) Present human interference with the nonhuman world is excessive, and the situation is rapidly worsening.

(6) Policies must therefore be changed. These policies affect basic economic, technological, and ideological structures. The resulting situation will be deeply different from the present.

(7) The ideological change will be mainly that of appreciating life quality (dwelling in the situation of inherent value) rather than adhering to an increasingly higher standard of living. There will be a profound awareness of the difference between bigness and greatness.

(8) Those who subscribe to the foregoing points have an obligation directly or indirectly to try and implement the necessary changes.[6]

It is important to notice that the very first point is a rejection of anthropocentrism in favor of ecocentrism. Anthropocentrism is the idea that humans are superior to or more valuable than the rest of nature. Ecocentrism rejects anthropocentrism by putting entire ecosystems at the center of focus instead of only humans. Naess is clearly seeking to move away from anthropocentrism toward ecocentrism, although what this would actually mean for humans is highly debated and controversial. In the next chapter, we will explore more fully what it would mean to treat entire ecosystems as valuable rather than humans only.

It is also worth noticing here that while Naess is resisting anthropocentrism, he does not seem to fully embrace an ecocentric position that might treat humans as equal to the rest of nature: his third point insists that humans should not diminish ecological "richness and diversity except to satisfy vital needs." This does imply that humans must reign in their uncontrolled destruction of the world, but seems to allow some degree of potential destruction as necessary for "vital needs." He recommends smaller human populations and less human domination of nature but does seem to think humans can establish sufficiently sustainable relationships with nature.

Moreover, Naess does not outline specific policy suggestions here. Deep ecologists are not afraid to suggest specific policy changes (as we will see in the next chapter), but they do not think these changes will occur without fundamental rejection and alteration of the dominant paradigm. The suggestion—that philosophical and even spiritual changes must occur first and foremost at a fundamental level—flies directly in the face of the dominant paradigm, which is overwhelmingly inclined to treat environmental issues as technical issues with technical solutions. Not surprisingly, most politicians and scientists tend to ignore deep ecological approaches. It remains to be seen if there will be some breaking point that will result in fracturing the dominant paradigm.

5.5 SPIRITUALITY

Perhaps most jarring to the dominant paradigm, some deep ecologists turn not only to philosophy but also to spirituality. The claim here from deep ecologists is that the dominant paradigm is not only philosophically problematic but spiritually damaging. In modern life, we tend to be alienated from the world. Some deep ecologists believe that healing both the damaged environment and our own damaged selves requires reconnecting spiritually with the natural world:

> For deep ecology, the study of our place in the Earth household includes the study of ourselves as part of the organic whole. Going beyond a narrowly materialist scientific understanding of reality, the spiritual and material aspects of reality fuse together. While the leading intellectuals of the dominant worldview have tended to view religion as "just superstition," and have looked upon ancient spiritual practice and enlightenment, such as found in Zen Buddhism, as essentially subjective, the search for deep ecological consciousness is the search for a more objective consciousness and state of being through an active deep questioning and meditative process and way of life...
>
> A nurturing nondominating society can help in the "real work" of becoming a whole person. The "real work" can be summarized symbolically as the realization of "self-in-Self" where "self" stands for organic wholeness. The process of the full unfolding of the self can be also summarized by the phrase, "No one is saved until we are all saved," where the phrase "one" includes not only me, an individual human, but all humans, whales, grizzly bears, whole rain forest ecosystems, mountain and river, the tiniest microbes in the soil, and so on.[7]

In this passage, Buddhist concerns with overcoming the self are combined with environmental concerns. The claim here is that overcoming atomistic or hyperindividualistic self-understanding requires seeing oneself as part of a larger organic whole and seeking to care for this greater whole instead of only the atomistic self. Ostensibly, this would help heal both the alienated modern individual and the environment and promote a more nurturing relationship between humans and the world around them.

5.6 DEEP ECOLOGY AND ECOCENTRISM

While deep ecologists seek to move away from anthropocentrism toward a more ecocentric approach, ecocentrism is not limited to deep ecologists. One famous example of an ecocentric approach that predates deep ecology is Aldo Leopold's land ethic. Thus, while most if not all deep ecologists are committed to ecocentrism, not all ecocentrists are deep ecologists. As such, it makes sense to present ecocentrism as a new chapter, even though there is much overlap between these approaches. Because of these connections, I will delay assessing deep ecology until after the presentation of ecocentrism in the next chapter.

5.7 QUESTIONS FOR DISCUSSION

1. Deep ecology suggests that many current environmental efforts are not radical enough. Do you agree? Why or why not?
2. Why would deep ecologists turn to Asian and Native American philosophy? Is this a good idea in your opinion? Why? Why not?
3. Deep ecology also claims that the current environmental crisis is also a spiritual crisis and that it would require spiritual solutions. Why might some resist this? Do you think they are correct? Why or why not?

5.8 FURTHER READING

The original articulation of deep ecology starts with Arne Naess's 1973 paper "The Shallow and the Deep, Long-Range Ecology Movement." Devall and Sessions's *Deep Ecology: Living as if Nature Mattered* is the classic book-length study of deep ecology. Fritjof Capra's *The Web of Life: A New Scientific Understanding of Living Systems* is an interesting example of attempting to combine spirituality with science. *Deep Ecology for the Twenty-First Century: Readings on the Philosophy and Practice of the New Environmentalism* is the classic anthology of deep ecological writings and includes responses to critics.

Notes

1 Devall, Bill. "The Deep Ecology Movement." *National Resources Journal*, 20/2 (1980), 219–303.

2 Ibid.

3 Naess, Arne. "The Deep Ecological Movement: Some Philosophical Perspectives." *Philosophical Inquiry* 8, no. 102 (1986).

4 This is not a direct quotation of Naess but my summary of his discussion.

5 Devall, Bill. "The Deep Ecology Movement." *National Resources Journal*, 20/2 (1980), 219–303.

6 Naess, Arne. "The Deep Ecological Movement: Some Philosophical Perspectives." *Philosophical Inquiry* 8, no. 102 (1986).

7 Devall, Bill, and George Sessions. *Deep Ecology: Living as if Nature Mattered.* (Layton, UT: Gibbs Smith, 2007), 66–67.

6

ECOCENTRISM AND THE WILDERNESS DEBATE

This chapter is a continuation of the last—deep ecology seeks to move away from anthropocentrism toward ecocentrism. But there are thinkers that predate deep ecology that articulated ecocentric positions. Separating deep ecology and ecocentrism, as is done here, recognizes that there is no complete overlap between them. Additionally, this chapter also includes a discussion of the wilderness debate, which is not an environmental philosophy so much as a debate within environmental philosophy that is connected to deep ecology and ecocentrism. The wilderness debate illustrates some of the tensions of an ecocentric position.

6.1 ALDO LEOPOLD AND THE LAND ETHIC

Aldo Leopold, a key figure in environmentalism, articulated a holistic understanding of ecosystems and a corresponding holistic land ethic. His influential *A Sand County Almanac* (1949) was influenced by early ecology but predates the philosophical approach of deep ecology.[1] Unlike earlier celebrants of wilderness such as Henry David Thoreau or John Muir, who tended to extoll the virtues of wilderness *for* humans, Leopold argued for a less anthropocentric defense of wilderness.

Leopold lived during an era of massive, systematic destruction of wilderness. As settlers moved west across the United States, they logged forests, hunted animals to extinction, and attempted to colonize Indigenous Peoples.

69

It is difficult for readers of our time to understand the abundance of life in the Americas before the arrival of Western settlers: the great plains were a kind of American Serengeti: clouds of birds darkened the skies, bears roamed everywhere, huge forests blanketed much of the US and Canada. Not only were these lands and animals treated as objects of ethical inferiority to humans, and thus available for settlers' use, but they were often killed off with little to no understanding of how they were interconnected. Wolves, for example, were destroyed to stop their predation on cattle with little understanding of how this would affect other animals.

What Leopold came to understand was that wolves were related to everything else in an ecosystem. If wolves were killed off, there would be more elk, which would eat more vegetation, which would alter the ecosystem in myriad ways. There is a fundamental shift in thinking here from caring about some species (or not caring at all) to caring about the land and all the species that are interrelated and connected. While duck hunters might seek to preserve wetlands so they can keep hunting, the wetlands will dry out if the river is damned or the ducks might disappear if the environment is too altered. Since everything is interconnected, those species we value or those environments we prefer cannot stand alone and depend on other species and systems for their continued existence. Beyond this, Leopold claimed wilderness was valuable in itself, not just in terms of how and to what degree it was useful to humans. As such, he advocated for wilderness preservation and sought to raise awareness of how humans are interconnected and dependent on their environment.

Leopold was critical of industrial society and did believe that humans needed to see themselves as a part of larger biotic communities, but he didn't tend to go as far as deep ecologists. Thus, we get an ecocentric land ethic but without as strong a denunciation of the dominant paradigm or a search for inspiration and spiritual sustenance in non-Western sources.

6.2 ECOCENTRISM

As we saw in the last chapter, ecocentrism stands in contrast to anthropocentrism. It seeks to value entire ecosystems instead of only or primarily humans. But it remains to be seen what this actually entails: What would it mean to take seriously the idea that nonhuman life is not inferior or less important than human life?

Take, for example, what it would mean to take seriously the value of large mammals such as, for example, jaguars. The major issue jaguars face is loss of habitat. They need large territories. But much of these were converted into farmland and left only fragments of wilderness that are not adequate for jaguars to thrive on in the long-term. A shallow approach may seek to create captive breeding programs, perhaps create some more wilderness areas, perhaps try to establish ecotourism, profits from which could help jaguars. But these efforts are inadequate. The fact of the matter is that jaguars need much more territory. An anthropocentric perspective will say that we should not sacrifice farmlands or undermine the economy to help jaguars, while an ecocentric perspective will recognize that jaguars are connected to entire ecosystems and that the human alteration and destruction of these ecosystems is affecting many plant and animal species in ways that are unethical and unacceptable.

The deep ecologist George Sessions adopts this line of argumentation and asks: What would have to change if we took the health of ecosystems seriously? He suggests that humankind would have to completely reorganize itself in order to make this possible. Like jaguars, flourishing ecosystems need time and space, but too many ecosystems are being fragmented and altered to remain healthy. If we adopted an ecocentric perspective, we would need to relocate humans in order to create more wild spaces. Sessions outlines a plan whereby one third of the land is allocated as wilderness and left completely alone, one third is mostly "free" (with limited human habitation and intervention), and one third is devoted to humans and the agriculture they require.[2] The claim is that this is the kind of space and freedom ecosystems need to grow and evolve. Obviously, few ecosystems currently have this kind of space.

It is interesting to see the reaction of students when they read this plan. Some find it outlandish, some find it intriguing, and some like the idea, but most agree that it is never going to be put into practice. Why? Because humans just aren't willing to make these kinds of sacrifices. I ask them to put aside the question of feasibility and then ask if this sort of thing makes sense from an ecocentric perspective. Many think that it does and even suggest that it is something of a compromise in those terms—it is still letting one species monopolize one third of the land. In this sense, Sessions's proposal can also function as a thought experiment, encouraging us to imagine what it would take if we did adopt an ecocentric approach. If anything, it reveals how uncritically anthropocentric most of our modern institutions, practices, self-understanding, and ethics are.

Much of the tension surrounding deep ecology and other environmental movements concerns this question: Who do environmental movements, efforts, and legislation aim to help? Frustratingly, it has proven extremely difficult to get humans to value the environment. Appeals concerning environmental issues tend to be framed in terms of how humans are affected: rising seas will inundate many coastal cities; therefore, you should care and we should make some changes before it is too late. The problem here, according to deep ecology and ecocentrists, is that framing the issue in these terms may itself be contributing to these problems—mass extinction and climate change are cast as important in terms of their effects on humans. This is primarily the reason why this text began with metaphysical questions about the nature of reality: perhaps we need to see the world around us as alive, meaningful, and valuable in order to care for it in the right ways. As long as we dwell in a dead universe that we must technologically manipulate for our own benefit, the environmental crisis will only worsen.

6.3 THE WILDERNESS DEBATE AND THE PROBLEM OF COLONIALISM

These kinds of questions led to an extended debate among environmental thinkers about wilderness. What exactly is it? What should we do with the wilderness that remains? How? What needs to change?

As straightforward as it seems at first, it quickly became apparent that "wilderness" is a fraught term that comes from a particular cultural background and carries specific baggage as a result. "Wild" and "wilderness" in Western thought stands in contrast to "cultivated," "culture," and "civilization." Traditionally, for Western thinkers, wilderness was seen as bad and opposed to civilization. Wilderness had to be limited, kept at bay, managed, and controlled. Only later, with the Romantic writers, do we see a reversal in which wilderness is treated as something wonderful and sublime that can offer a balm to the damaged humans of modern civilization (as John Muir famously said).[3] Romantic wilderness is something that one can leave the city to visit and enjoy. Note that the distinction between "civilization" and "wilderness" remains the same whichever one is valued. But the particular moral and aesthetic valences that surround "civilization" and "wilderness" here are not universal: some cultures see no distinction between civilization and wilderness at all.

As we saw with Sessions, one of the pushes of deep ecologists and environmentalists of the 1970s and 1980s was to establish more wilderness areas. But how should this be done and how should they be managed? In the US, wilderness areas are managed by various government agencies that have inconsistent approaches.[4] The forest service treats wilderness as a resource and sees their purpose as managing forests. This means that they do allow logging, but they limit how much is done and how. The idea here is that these resources should be used but in a way that doesn't deplete them. The national parks service, on the other hand, doesn't allow logging. This makes for a remarkable difference at the boundaries of National Parks, with the side that was not parkland often having smaller trees or clear-cut trees and the park side having ancient or larger second-growth trees. The differences can be clearly seen on Google Earth.

Carl Talbot argues that even though national parks may not allow logging or the kinds of developments allowed on forest service land, nonetheless the "wilderness" experience of national parks is often treated as a commodity. He quotes a spokesperson at Zion Nation Park: "There's a market for this. The one and a half million people who visit Zion each year won't have to sweat or get their heart rate above a wheelchair level. Whole busloads can come to Springdale, have the Zion experience and be in Las Vegas that night."[5] Talbot claims that the national parks serving as an escapist commodity actually reinforces the industrial, capitalist activity going on everywhere else. Tired workers can escape to the highly managed, "safe" wilderness of national parks, take their selfies, get rejuvenated, and return to their jobs on Monday, ready to go at it again. The disturbing result is that, yet again, wilderness ideologically serves civilization: for some, these "preserved" areas indicate the magnanimity of civilization, preserving it for our enjoyment and for the fortunate animals that have been saved; for others, it is a play place; and for another group, it is an alien place that is wonderful, but ultimately reaffirms the projects of modernity instead of challenging them. On Talbot's account, then, our efforts to preserve and manage wilderness can often end up commodifying it and serving the very forces that have been destroying it.

Most concerning is the ways that the use and misuse of wilderness can be colonial. As this point is particularly important, let's make it clear: in terms of world history, colonialism refers to one country taking over another and turning it into a colony. The initial wave of modern colonialism came in the 1500s–1600s. Spain and Portugal colonized Latin America. Britain colonized what would become the USA and Canada. A second wave of colonialism occurred in the 1800s when European countries extensively colonized Africa and parts of Asia. Japan also colonized Korea and parts of China. In some cases, colonialism involved the outright genocide of aboriginal peoples. In most cases, it meant the exploitation of natural resources and peoples, destruction of local cultures, enslavement, "modernization," and reeducation. "Modernization" refers to the process of destroying local cultures and practices and replacing them with "modern" or Western practices. Thus, colonialism involved a kind of brainwashing or indoctrination that denigrated non-Western practices and traditions while praising and enforcing Western ones, often with the goal of creating populations willing to work for and buy products from the West. "Postcolonialism" includes efforts to undo this damage.

Wilderness is both something that can be colonized and something that can be intertwined with colonialism. Let's look at two examples, one from

Thomas Birch and one from Ramachandra Guha. Birch argues that Western practices have incarcerated wilderness.[6] He points to American narratives about wilderness creation that praise America for its progressive and forward-thinking preservation of wilderness and argues that these efforts are not made in good faith. Like Talbot, Birch argues that wilderness is often turned into a useful foil for modern civilization. Just as animals can be imprisoned in zoos and observed with fascination and perhaps even fear by civilized masses, so too is wilderness articulated as a wild object that we rule over and that we benevolently maintain in preserved spaces. These wild spaces serve as a reminder of the comforts and ingenuity of modern civilizations. If for some reason we start to dislike modern life, we can always say to ourselves "But this is so much better than having to fight off bears and lions." Furthermore, the managed "wild" spaces of places like national parks illustrate our power over nature and our magnanimity. From the least wild, managed "wilderness" to the most wild, free "wilderness": these places are not allowed to speak on their own terms, but are turned into objects that serve our cultural and ideological needs.

The problem is not only the colonization of wilderness for humans, but other colonial effects that come from efforts to settle the wilderness. Thus, Guha, writing from a "third world" perspective, pointed out that the deep ecologist dream of creating more wild spaces may make sense in North America, but it doesn't in India.[7] According to Guha, one of the major problems in creating wilderness areas in India is that there are few areas without human inhabitants. Thus, creating wilderness areas requires displacing long-established human communities. (For example, countless Native Americans were killed or forcibly removed from what would become US national parks.) Furthermore, many of these wilderness areas tend to become tourist spots for wealthy Indians and foreign visitors. In other words, wilderness creation in India too often destroys the traditional livelihood of poor farmers and tends to benefit the wealthy instead. Viewed from this perspective, we have Western foreigners telling India what to do with land (preserve wildlife and wilderness) and more often than not benefiting wealthy Indians: this certainly seems like more colonialism. Guha argues that instead of Western environmentalists coming into India and telling it what to do, they should look to the damage being done by Global North consumerism and arms dealing. More damage is done by Western consumer practices and Western-funded and -supplied wars than by small farmers. Guha's claim is not that deep ecology is bad—he is actually quite sympathetic to ecocentrism—but that it needs to be more self-critical, much more sensitive to the potential colonial implications of wilderness and other environmental projects. It also needs to be much more careful in how it seeks "answers" from non-Western intellectual and cultural traditions. This is too often superficial, appropriative, and reductive.

The wilderness debate reveals the complexity of environmental issues. We may seek to do something that seems obviously good (like creating wilderness areas for endangered Indian wildlife) only to discover there are colonial consequences (like the forced migration of impoverished small farmers). It is clear from Naess's principles of deep ecology and discussion of the differences between deep and shallow ecology (discussed in the last chapter) that deep ecologists and ecocentrists have been concerned about the potential colonial consequences of radical environmental change. The wilderness debate shows that these concerns must extend to key environmental terms like "wilderness" and requires a postcolonial historical and cultural sensitivity.

6.4 ASSESSING DEEP ECOLOGY AND ECOCENTRISM

Where does this leave deep ecology and ecocentrism as environmental theories? Although deep ecology was perhaps the dominant environmental approach in the 1970s and 1980s, for some nowadays it has become old-fashioned. Why? And what does this mean for students of environmental philosophy today?

Many environmentalists are sympathetic to ecocentrism. The difficult question is how far we can or should go with it. A position that truly considered nonhuman life as being equally valuable to human life might potentially have some extreme implications. What if humankind cannot prove capable of applying limits to its own growth and consumerism? Is it likely to eat out the Earth from under itself, destroying our planet for all beings both human and nonhuman? Naess thought we should limit human population but seems to believe that humans and nonhumans can survive together. However, based on the worsening environmental crisis, some might conclude this is not the case. If humans are the problem, then it is easy to imagine someone concluding that humans have to go. While few openly voice that conclusion, critics have labeled such efforts "eco-fascist." The worry here is that ecocentrism could lead to deep pessimism about and even action against humankind. Of course, this is something of a fallacious slippery slope argument—moving away from anthropocentrism toward ecocentrism does not imply embracing "eco-fascism," and at times the term is thrown at anyone who suggests anything radical, especially anything that seeks to slow the economy for environmental purposes. Hence the derogatory term "eco-fascism" risks becoming a meaningless refrain used as some employ the word "socialism": useful for scaring people but at most a cheap reactionary insult. This actually hides the genuine tension between anthropocentrism and ecocentrism.

While many environmentalists remain sympathetic to some degree about ecocentrism, deep ecology has less influence than it used to, for a variety of reasons. First, and perhaps sadly, many theories in the humanities tend to come and go simply because people run out of things to say about them and become attracted by newer theories. To the extent that this is the case, it would not reflect on the quality of deep ecology as an approach, but rather on often-fickle academic trends. Second, as we have seen with the wilderness debate, deep ecology elicited serious philosophical questions and concerns: How would it work in so-called "third world" (Global South) countries? Does it run the risk of being a colonial approach? These concerns do not necessarily undermine a deep ecological approach but do point to tensions that warrant careful attention. Third, as Naess was already aware, the radicality of deep ecology and its willingness to challenge the Western status quo means that it faces trenchant resistance. Deep ecologically minded thinkers risked being sidelined and ignored by more mainstream scientists unless they accepted or compromised heavily with the norms and expectations of the dominant paradigm. Frankly, it is easier to try and work within the system than to challenge it wholesale. Sadly, it appears that many environmental thinkers have had to settle for more "practical" approaches. In other words, the difficulties inherent in deep ecology may lead many to settle for shallow ecology.

Lastly, some find the spiritual aspect of deep ecology unappealing. Some contemporary environmentalists may find deep ecology's efforts at spirituality dated, especially if these come across as "new-agey" or "hippyish." This is not to say that such efforts are misguided; they may have a residue of 1970s and 1980s countercultural spirituality that simply might not fit contemporary preferences. In other words, it might be an aesthetic or preferential assessment, one that may very well reflect the awkwardness toward spirituality that often exists in a pluralistic secular society. It could also indicate the alienation with the world that some deep ecologists sought to address.

We can learn from both the successes and failures of deep ecology and ecocentrism. Deep ecology teaches us that truly addressing the environmental crisis may require far more radical responses than the standard shallow approaches. It requires carefully and critically thinking about the status quo and the dominant paradigm. This involves thinking through the historically and culturally charged terrain and language of environmental issues and striving to be alert to the potential colonial aspects of this work. Ecocentrism alerts us to the need to challenge the superficial anthropocentrism of much of Western thought and practice.

6.5 QUESTIONS FOR DISCUSSION

1. What is anthropocentrism? What are examples of this in everyday language and practice?
2. What are the implications of ecocentrism if pushed to the extreme? What do you make of these implications?
3. Creating more wilderness areas seems like a good thing. Why is doing so important? Despite the potential positive effects, some have voiced concerns about these efforts. Why? Do you agree with these concerns?
4. Some environmentalists may shy away from deep ecology and ecocentrism because their radicality makes them difficult to implement. But then we get stuck where we began: making only superficial changes. Given these tensions, what strategies do you think make sense?

6.6 FURTHER READING

Aldo Leopold's *Sand County Almanac* is a classic text for thinking about a land ethic instead of an anthropocentric one. As deep ecologists advocate for ecocentrism, readers wishing learn more about it can consult Sessions, Devall, and Naess. Much of the discussion about wilderness can be found in *The Great New Wilderness Debate*.

Notes

1 Leopold, Aldo. *A Sand County Almanac: And Sketches Here and There* (New York: Oxford University Press, 2020).
2 Sessions, George. "Ecocentrism, Wilderness and Global Systems Protection." In Oelschlaeger, Max, ed., *The Wilderness Condition: Essays on Environment and Civilization* (Covelo, CA: Island Press, 1992).
3 Muir, John. *Our National Parks* (Boston, MA: Houghton, Mifflin and Company, 1901).
4 Sessions, George. "Ecocentrism, Wilderness and Global Systems Protection." In Oelschlaeger, Max, ed., *The Wilderness Condition: Essays on Environment and Civilization* (Covelo, CA: Island Press, 1992).
5 Talbot, Carl. "The Wilderness Narrative and the Cultural Logic of Capitalism." In Callicot, J. Baird and Michael P. Nelson, eds., *The Great New Wilderness Debate* (Athens, GA: University of Georgia Press, 1998).
6 Birch, Thomas H. "The Incarceration of Wilderness: Wilderness Areas as Prisons." In Callicot, J. Baird and Michael P. Nelson, eds., *The Great New Wilderness Debate* (Athens, GA: University of Georgia Press, 1998).
7 Guha, Ramachandra. "Radical American Environmentalism and Wilderness Preservation: A Third World Critique." In Callicot, J. Baird, and Michael P. Nelson, eds., *The Great New Wilderness Debate* (Athens, GA: University of Georgia Press, 1998).

7

ECOFEMINISM

Ecofeminism combines feminist philosophy and environmental philosophy. Ecofeminists claim not only that feminism has important insights for environmental philosophy, but also that the two working together form a uniquely compelling position. To understand ecofeminism, we need to understand that feminism is not a monolithic tradition as well as some of the tensions among various feminisms.

7.1 FEMINISMS

Feminist philosophy and feminism are very complex traditions—so much so that we should perhaps speak of feminisms. There are different ways to distinguish these feminisms. I will use Eva Kittay's analysis in her *Love's Labor*.[1] Kittay points out that perhaps *the* fundamental concern of feminism has been and continues to be equality. Feminists concerned with equality have pointed out that men often treat women differently than they do other men in ways that are unfair and lead to unequal opportunities. Historically, women have not been not allowed to vote, hold public office, work in certain jobs, serve in the military, etc. And even when women had obtained the right to vote, they were still often discouraged from participating in politics and from working, and were often forced to remain in the domestic sphere. Thus, 1960s and 1970s feminism focused on gaining equal rights and opportunities for women. It also focused on the gender binary of men and women, which often involved highlighting that men and women are not that different and should be treated similarly instead of differently.

In the late 1970s and early 1980s, however, some feminists began to emphasize that certain differences between men and women were being ignored—to the detriment of women. As women began working in far greater numbers, many found that pregnancy limited their options. Employers, for example, might choose a less qualified man out of fear that a more qualified woman might quit her job if she became pregnant. Not only were women discriminated against for the sheer possibility of becoming pregnant, but as they had no parental leave, getting pregnant often meant getting fired. In terms of this issue, therefore, men and women could not be treated the same. To do so often meant that, among other things, men's bodily experience was considered normal or the default standard.[2] Pregnancy was outside of this "normal" and was seldom taken into account by the expectations of public and professional spaces. To prevent discrimination against women, laws and expectations had to be altered to create a space in which women were protected in light of their differences from men.

Some feminists argued that these differences extend further than mere bodily differences. The psychologist Carol Gilligan noticed that men and women tended to answer questions about ethics and moral action differently.[3] Men tended to value and prefer answers to moral problems that were phrased as abstract rules or principles, whereas women tended to value and prefer answers to moral problems that paid attention to particular circumstances and the relations of the individuals involved. Although Gilligan did not try to provide a scientific or historic answer as to why these differences occur (in other words, she didn't try to answer the question of whether this was due to nature or nurture), she did seek to understand the ramifications of these differences. She argued that the moral reasoning of women indicated an *ethics of care* that differed from the moral reasoning of men. She and other feminists argued that these moral differences are deeply significant and have striking social and political implications. The feminist care ethics that emerged critiqued the cold utilitarianism of much of contemporary moral thought in favor of a more relational, less abstract, more caring approach.

Notice that "equality" feminism and "difference" feminism have divergent goals and emphases. Among other things, the former aimed for equality for women by rejecting the ways that supposed differences between men and women justified limiting women's activities. But "difference" feminists argued that there existed significant differences that should be understood and considered instead of dismissed or downplayed. Almost as soon as "difference" feminism appeared, it ran into criticisms that it was in danger of essentializing women. The worry here was that in emphasizing the differences between men and women, "difference" feminism was falling into the trap of claiming that there are certain features that are related to men or masculinity and others related to women or femininity. This criticism was especially voiced by nonwhite feminists, who pointed out that these descriptions of men or women often didn't fit their experience. In other words, black and South Asian feminists especially pointed out that the discourse of difference feminism was often driven by white academic women and that some of the distinctions they were drawing fit a certain socioeconomic category of white women more than something universal or "essential". The diversity critique offered by nonwhite women pointed out that there were far more pivotal differences than just sexuality (such as race, class, gender, and culture), and that whatever differences we might find between men and women were sure to vary by class, culture, and so forth, not to mention the omission of non-binary individuals. The diversity critique has come to stress "intersectionality"—the fact that any theory must take into account these many factors and how they affect each other in unique situations.

Kittay also gives an account of the dominance critique, an approach that aims to analyze and end male dominance, and of the dependency critique (her own approach), which seeks to understand the implications of our interdependency in contrast with our modern self-identity and political organization that centers on our supposed independence.[4]

Ecofeminists come from each of these traditions. Despite these differences, however, one of the fundamental claims of all ecofeminists is that they have "epistemic privilege"—that their position in patriarchal society allows them to see things that men (especially those in power) might not see. I explain this claim in the next section.

7.2 STANDPOINT THEORY

Standpoint theory comes from Marx, who claimed that the proletariat, by virtue of their situation in industrial capitalism, are in a better place to understand the reality (the injustices) of that system.[5] Those who had been driven off their traditional farmlands into factories saw the failures of industrial capitalism, while the bourgeois factory owners overlooked, failed to see, or excused the cruelties of capitalism. For Marx, the proletariat has epistemic privilege—special knowledge about what is happening.

For many ecofeminists, then, the environmentally-minded feminist has epistemic privilege, including about environmental issues. This is because both women and the environment are objects of patriarchal control in modern society. Carol Adams, for example, argues that both women and animals (meat) are treated by men as objects to be desired, dismembered, and consumed.[6] She shows examples in advertising of meat being sold with sexualized language or images of women being objectified and treated like meat. In Adams's view, male identity becomes tied to eating meat and controlling or using women, and for many men the association of meat eating and chasing women is taken for granted. She argues that women are far more likely to recognize and understand the depth of the problem than are men. Adams is not claiming that all women will understand this, but that because many women have been and/or have seen other women treated this way and subject to this language, they are more likely to recognize and understand these connections.

The claim of epistemic privilege, then, is one that indicates the need not just for feminist analysis of environmental issues, but for an ecofeminism that integrates feminist and environmental concerns. This claim is not only relevant to industrialized countries, but also industrializing countries. Many environmental problems affect women in particular. These might include access to water (often carried by women); replacement of traditional gardening, farming practices and commons with privatized monocropping; food insecurity; pollution, etc.[7] Many traditional practices reflect women (and men) interacting with their environments for many generations and developing certain forms of expertise that have been ignored by Western "experts."[8] Too often these practices are ignored in favor of modern agricultural methods or more "scientific" methods. Thus, women and children are often disproportionately affected by environmental problems *and* their traditional knowledge is rarely appreciated. Too often the efficacy of modern social change is judged by increases in GDP, while it is often women and children who feel the brunt of these changes and therefore have a fuller picture of the situation. As Vandana Shiva puts it, "The marginalization of women and the destruction of biodiversity go hand in hand. Diversity is the price paid in the patriarchal mode of progress which pushed inexorably towards monocultures, uniformity, and homogeneity...It helps to look at dominant structures from below."[9] When we do so from the perspective of the complex, diversified practices of rural women, we discover that modern agricultural practices that are supposedly productive and driven by superior knowledge instead appear unproductive (producing a lot of one crop instead of a much richer, community-connected, and immediately useful variety of crops) and primitive (simplistic and streamlined).

7.3 ECOFEMINISM: AGAINST DOMINATION, TOWARD CARE

Not surprisingly, one of the major concerns of ecofeminists is the domination of women and of the natural world. In Chapter 3, we examined Carolyn Merchant's historical and philosophical analysis of *The Death of Nature*.

Merchant pointed to the shift in metaphors that took place with the rise of modern capitalism and science: the image of Mother Earth was increasingly replaced with the image of a machine. The gendered metaphor of the earth being our mother shaped how human relations to it are understood: mining appears as an avaricious violation, even rape. A machine, on the other hand, requires and calls for intervention if it is not working adequately. Merchant claims that the cultural domination of women (witches) runs parallel to the scientific domination of nature.

Merchant connects women, nature, and science in a way that directly contradicts our standard narratives about science. As we saw above, one of the key strains in feminist critique is the "dominance" critique. While ostensibly coming from a feminist perspective, feminist critiques of "dominance" are not limited to the treatment of women, but often seek to show how overlapping forms of dominance affect not only women but other marginalized and dominated groups. Thus, Marxist feminists examine how capitalism affects the exploited class and women. Postcolonial feminists examine how colonialism affects the colonized and women. Ecofeminists examine the exploitation of the environment and women: "Women must see that there can be no liberation for them and no solution to the ecological crisis within a society whose fundamental model of relationships continues to be one of domination. They must unite the demands of the women's movement with those of the ecological movement to envision a radical reshaping of the basic socioeconomic relations and the underlying values of this society."[10] But since these forms of domination overlap we often find feminist works like Merchant's that connect issues that seem disparate at first and connect things that may seem unrelated (science—supposedly a neutral method) to complex forms of contemporary exploitation (women and the environment).

Take for example the relation of toxic masculinity to environmentalism. Toxic masculinity is a fruitful term that describes the ways that certain kinds of masculinity are harmful both for men and for women. It is meant to emphasize how modern ideals of masculinity can lead to a rejection of emotion except anger (which leads to a lack of emotional intelligence), a tendency toward aggression and violence, a misguided sense of privilege, a harmful aversion to things that are perceived to be feminine or "girly," etc. Interestingly, it turns out that toxic masculinity plays a role in men's attitudes toward environmental issues. A recent study showed that merely having the name "green" (in the sense of "environmentally friendly") applied to something meant that many men were less likely to associate with it.[11] As silly as it sounds, "green" is associated with weakness, compromise, and caring, whereas a real man is strong, uncompromising, and stoic.

While ecofeminism alerts us to the complex forces of domination in modern society, some ecofeminists have also sought alternatives to the domineering approach of modernity, including care ethics. Recall that care ethics was an ethical theory that grew out of "difference" feminism and sought an alternative to the cold, principle-, and rule-based ethics of utilitarianism and Kantian ethics that have been the dominant ethical theories in modernity. Care ethics seeks to foster a relational, situational, careful approach. Take for example Sarah Ruddick's *Maternal Thinking*.[12] In this work, Ruddick examines mothering (an activity she clarifies is not limited to women) and the ways it may contribute to a philosophy of peace. She is *not* claiming that mothers are inherently peacemakers—in fact, she rejects the "myth of maternal peacefulness" since historically many mothers have supported wars.[13] Rather, she claims that certain caring efforts of mothers to create "preservative love" and "fostering growth" for children can be applied to goals of peace.[14] Ruddick goes to great lengths to avoid equating love and caring with women only, but some feminists such as Gilligan would point out that while we need not claim that men are essentially more violent and women essentially more peaceful, we see in the moral commitments of men and women in certain communities definite tendencies toward violence and caring. The women in Gilligan's studies evince an ethics of care that she thinks is politically important.

It is easy to see why some ecofeminists call for an ethics of care with regard to the environment and speak of "ecocaring."[15] While there are different visions of what this would look like, it is fair to say it would run counter to toxic masculinity's rejection of helping the environment because to do so is unmanly. Instead of taking the individual as the starting point, the community, including the environment, is both start and end points. Instead of seeing love, connection, and caring as inferior or unmanly, one should see them as deeply human, fulfilling, and needed. Instead of seeing existence as competition, one should seek cooperation. If this seems saccharine, introspect why. Ecocaring radically challenges many of the underlying imperatives of modern life in ways that are sophisticated and powerful.

7.4 CRITICISMS

Ecofeminism ran into some of the same problems as difference feminism. As some ecofeminists tried to work out an alternative to patriarchal society, they were accused of invoking essentialist images of women. Noel Sturgeon gives examples of some of the kinds of images that were invoked by some ecofeminists or used to illustrate ecofeminist anthologies.[16] These included the "white goddess" and Indigenous imagery. The "white goddess" imagery often uses new age Celtic druid art and portrays a powerful, hippy-like white goddesses with flowing hair. Indigenous imagery of women in what was understood to be traditional dress, or Indigenous art such as dream catchers, also make appearances. Sturgeon points out not only the obvious problem of appropriating Indigenous imagery, but also the problem of whiteness being taken as a default. The point is not an aesthetic judgment, but the significance of this kind of imagery and how it reflected a predominantly white audience. As we saw earlier, nonwhite feminists criticized how some "difference" feminists described the differences between men and women. These descriptions did not always fit nonwhite experiences and left "difference" feminists open to accusations of essentialism. The diversity critique showed both the danger of describing the way "men" or "women" are, as if there were not great variation, and the need to adopt an intersectional approach that recognizes the complex overlap of race, gender, sexuality, class, culture, etc.

Sturgeon argues, however, that these lessons do not mean that we can function without generalizations, that it is wrong to draw distinctions, or that we can only analyze very narrow situations. In other words, we don't have to throw out the insights of ecofeminism because some of its advocates have made reductive or essentialist claims. Historically, however, it does seem that the diversity critique did take some of the wind out of the sails of ecofeminism. Furthermore, as we saw at the end of the last chapter, the fate of theories in the humanities is often a result of academic trends. Movements are exciting for a while but get worked over and become boring. I am not saying this to diminish the importance of diversity critiques, but simply to point out that the waxing and waning of academic theories shouldn't mean we dismiss theories because they are older or not trendy.

If some environmental philosophers are dismissive of ecofeminism, they tend to be so along the lines just outlined. But it is also clear that gender does play an important role in environmental issues and that we need feminist and ecofeminist voices to keep us alert to these issues.

7.5 QUESTIONS FOR DISCUSSION
1. Why might it make sense to speak of "feminisms" and not just "feminism"?
2. How do "equality" feminism and "difference" feminism differ? What is the significance of these differences? Which influenced ecofeminism and why?
3. What is standpoint theory? How do some feminists use it?
4. Why do ecofeminists think feminism is important for environmentalism?

5. What does it mean to essentialize women? Why was this criticism leveled at ecofeminism?

6. What is intersectionality? How does it help overcome essentialism?

7.6 FURTHER READING

There are many ecofeminism readers. Some, like *Ecofeminism: Feminist Intersections with Other Animals and the Earth* (ed. Adams and Gruen), make the necessity of intersectionality overt. One of the key texts for difference feminism and feminist care ethics is Carol Gilligan's *In a Different Voice*. Merchant's *The Death of Nature* (discussed in Chapter 3) explores the tensions among gender, nature, and science. Carol J. Adams's *The Sexual Politics of Meat* has become an important work for vegetarians and explores how the exploitation of women parallels the exploitation of animals. Patricia Hill Collins, best known for her book *Black Feminist Thought*, is another important figure for exploring black feminism and intersectionality.

Notes

1 Kittay, Eva Feder. *Love's Labor: Essays on Women, Equality and Dependency* (New York: Routledge, 1999).

2 Little, Margaret Olivia. "Why a Feminist Approach to Bioethics?" *Kennedy Institute of Ethics Journal*, 6.1 (1996), 1–18.

3 Gilligan, Carol. *In a Different Voice: Psychological Theory and Women's Development* (Cambridge, MA: Harvard University Press, 2009).

4 Kittay, Eva Feder. *Love's Labor: Essays on Women, Equality and Dependency* (New York: Routledge, 1999).

5 Tucker, Robert C., ed. *The Marx–Engels Reader* (New York: W.W. Norton, 1978).

6 Adams, Carol J. *The Sexual Politics of Meat: A Feminist-Vegetarian Critical Theory* (New York: Bloomsbury, 2015).

7 Gaard, Greta and Lori Gruen. "Ecofeminism: Toward Global Justice and Planetary Health." *Society and Nature*, 2 (1993), 1–35.

8 Curtin, Deane. "Women's Knowledge as Expert Knowledge: Indian Women and Ecodevelopment." In *Ecological Feminism: Multidisciplinary Perspectives*, ed. Karen Williams (Bloomington, IN: Indiana University Press, 1997).

9 Shiva, Vandana. "Women's Indigenous Knowledge and Biodiversity Conservation." *India International Centre Quarterly*, vol. 19, nos. 1–2 (Spring-Summer 1992), 205–14.

10 Radford Reuther, Rosemary. *New Woman, New Earth: Sexist Ideologies and Human Liberation* (Boston, MA: Beacon Press, 1995), 204.

11 Brough, Aaron R. and James E.B. Wilkie. "Men Resist Green Behavior as Unmanly." *Scientific American* (26 December 2017).

12 Ruddick, Sarah. *Maternal Thinking: Towards a Politics of Peace* (Boston, MA: Beacon Press, 1995).

13 Ibid., 219–21.

14 Ibid., 65–102.

15 Estévez-Saá, Margarita and María Jesús Lorenzo-Modia. *The Ethics and Aesthetics of Eco-caring: Contemporary Debates on Ecofeminism(s)* (New York: Routledge, 2020).

16 Sturgeon, Noel. "Naturalizing Race: Indigenous Women and White Goddesses." In Zimmermaman, Michael et al., eds., *Environmental Philosophy: From Animal Rights to Radical Ecology* (New York: Pearson, 2004), 228–51.

8

BIOREGIONALISM

Bioregionalism encourages us to live local and recover an intimate connection with community and place. It claims that doing so is critically important not only for the environment, but also for human wellbeing. This is a direct challenge to the environmentally troubling "homelessness" of modernity, which is the result not only of the disenchantment with the world in modern Western metaphysics discussed in the first section, but also of our ever increasing movement for jobs, work, school, and our increasing disconnection from the place we live in through technology and media.[1] In my own case, I was born in one place, moved to another when I was 5, again when I was 11, again when I was 19, then 21, then 25, then 30, then 35. When people ask me where I'm from, I'm not always sure what to answer. This is increasingly the case for many people, as the exigencies of ever-accelerating capitalism require the movement of both products and people. Not only may our employer ask us to travel for work, but many people change jobs multiple times. This constant movement of both people and things makes it difficult to connect with a specific place.

Connection with place is exactly what bioregionalism encourages us to do. But what does this entail? And what exactly are we connecting with?

8.1 WHAT IS A BIOREGION?

So, what is a bioregion? The word "bioregion" indicates a "life-territory." A bioregion is an area that shares a similar environment—in both the sense of flora and fauna—but also feel and personality. Thus, moving from one bioregion to another could involve a biotic shift, a new watershed, a distinct landform, a different culture and feel, separate orienting, sacred or "psyche-orienting" sites, and changing elevations.[2] Take for example the sky islands Arizona. These are isolated mountain peaks and ridges that rise out of the desert. At the base of the mountains, there are scorching deserts with Saguaros, Cholla cactus, diamondback rattlesnakes, and Gila monsters. But as one ascends the sky islands, the higher elevations feel completely different, with their pine trees, foxes, and bears. They really do feel like two different worlds although, of course, there are birds such as Rufus hummingbirds that visit both. Obviously, humans living in these places are going to develop unique practices. Higher altitudes may involve snow, while lower altitudes may involve hotter summers. Human habitation, food, movement, access to water, and so forth, will all be different and over time the resulting human cultures will also be quite different.

We see this in traditional food, clothing, art, and customs. Or just go to the grocery store and look at the many kinds of cheeses: Parmigiano-Reggiano, Roquefort, Gruyère, etc. These cheeses were developed in particular regions and are often made with milk from particular breeds of cows or goats who have eaten certain kinds of grasses. The same goes for "artisan" (i.e., traditional) wine, coffee, breads, meats, pastries, and so forth. These diverse foods all developed in particular bioregions with unique seasons, elevations, flora and fauna, and human cultures. We also have regional clothing, regional cultural and religious traditions, regional histories—all of which are shaped by place. Even today, some foods are so closely shaped by place that they are only "authentic" or "real" if they come from that place. Thus, champagne can only be called "champagne" if it is from Champagne, France. The same goes for Roquefort cheese. Interestingly, as the modern world has become more standardized and McDonaldized, "unique" traditional foods, some of which were originally cheap peasant foods, have become "gourmet" and highly expensive.

Fundamentally, then, a bioregion is shaped by flora, fauna, soil, seasons, and watersheds. But it is also shaped by the human practices that develop in these places—and this includes spiritual practices. As such, certain geographic features, animals, plants, rivers, etc., can garner cultural and spiritual significance that also demarcate bioregions. California is known for poppies, giant sequoias, and redwoods. The Mojave Desert is known for Joshua trees. Mt. Graham is sacred to the Apache. The Amazon, Nile, Ganges, and Mekong rivers are all immediately evocative. Similarly, certain peoples are immediately associated with certain landscapes: the Mongolians, the San (often problematically still referred to as 'African bushmen'), the Iroquois, the Greeks, aboriginal Australians.

It is possible then, in certain locations, to pass through multiple bioregions in a short period of time, especially when ascending or descending an elevation rapidly. High mountains can pass to lowlands, to coastlines, and to oceans—all distinct bioregions. Historically, each of these bioregions might have had different peoples with different cultures, languages, food, and religions.

8.2 DWELLERS IN THE LAND

Kirkpatrick Sale calls for us to dwell in the land.[3] The word "dwell" implies rootedness, living in a place for a long time, and being thoroughly familiar with it. What does this entail and why should we want to do it?

First, Sale claims we need to come to know the land. This means walking the landscapes, becoming familiar with the seasons, learning the names and behaviors of the plants and animals, and exploring local customs.

Second, we should learn the lore. This involves learning the history of a place, including both human history and nonhuman history. This helps imbue places, landmarks, animals, and plants with meaning. Here I will give a personal example. After reading and being inspired by Vine Deloria Jr., I committed myself to both learning the lore and seeking to know the land. This has changed how I experience the world around me. Having lived in various places in the Western US, I am now far more attentive to the destruction of Indigenous peoples and to the environments where I live. I know that I live on stolen and radically altered land. In fact, one place I lived was at the foot of a mountain, near the site of, and named after, a massacre of Native Americans. Once I had done the work of learning this history, I could never look at this mountain the same way and I would often experience the mountain looming over me, witnessing what had happened. Similarly, I learned about certain places around town that had once been sacred Indigenous sites. These places also came to bear witness to the past for me. Similarly, there are various threatened plant and animal species where I currently live. I have seen them, and they remind me of what once was. Having a sense of this environmental and human/cultural destruction is important not only to tamper down our personal hubris but to bring particular places to life. The rivers where I live have been extensively damaged, although efforts are being made by various governmental and non-governmental groups to redress the situation. Otters and salmon have returned to some of these locations. They are not just rivers for me anymore, but sites of environmental conflict and renewal. When I take my children to play in the Merced River, I think of the Sierra Mountains to the east and the Pacific Ocean to the west. The river connects me to nature, history, the land—even the future.

Third, Sale encourages us to develop the potential of place. This means working with the land—both its limitations and its potentials—and in turn allowing ourselves to be limited by the land. This could imply growing native plants, eating in season, farming in appropriate ways, developing sustainable practices, and so on. This is the sort of motivation behind contemporary efforts to eat, buy, and live local. Locally grown food can be bought from local farmers at farmers' markets and thus our money supports our own community.

Lastly, Sale argues that doing all this will help us liberate the self. This idea, in part, is based on the claim that many of us have been alienated from the land, from nature, and from local communities in modernity. Thus, dwelling in the land would reconnect us with that land and with the local community—hopefully, a community that is engaged in efforts to also reconnect with the land and history, and with its members. In communities where such efforts are ongoing, the community and those involved have a meaningful purpose that is hopefully mutually and environmentally affirming.

For Kirkpatrick Sale, it is also liberating for another reason, and that is his commitment to anarchism.

8.3 THE POLITICS OF BIOREGIONALISM

For some advocates of bioregionalism like Sale and Dodge, this affirmation of the local over the state or nation is anarchic. For many, anarchy sounds like chaos and riots, but here it means local governance. Like such accounts, bioregionalism is not only the demand that we seek to reconnect with place, but the radical sociopolitical demand that we reorganize ourselves by bioregions instead of states or provinces. This concern is born from the fact that a state may comprise many diverse environments and peoples, and that making laws, regulations, and establishing broad practices at the level of the state or nation may not respond adequately to the specific social, cultural, and environmental needs of different places.

Both Sale and Dodge worry that our modern society is driven by an "industrio-scientific paradigm" that privileges uniformity, transparency, profitability, and competition. Local communities and regional differences have been under attack throughout modernity. The ever-accelerating demand for profit seeks to eliminate the inefficiencies of smaller-scale local economies, language differences, and cultural differences. Bioregionalism seeks autonomy from the machinery of modernity. This is another part of the liberating potential of bioregionalism, according to Sale.

8.4 OPTING OUT: RADICAL HOMEMAKING

Bioregionalism is not alone in seeking to opt out of the "industrio-scientific paradigm" of modernity. The radical homemaking movement is quite similar to bioregionalism and is worth taking a moment to examine. Radical homemaking is a rejection of consumer society and a corresponding effort to make what we need instead of buying it. This implies a recovery of homemaking tasks that over time have been commodified.

The narrative of consumer culture is that being able to buy products instead of making them saves time and helps free women from the drudgery of homemaking. But radical homemaking points to the environmental, social, and political damage caused by consumerism. Like bioregionalism, radical homemaking suggests that consumerism leaves us alienated and disconnected from our environment and from each other. There is inherent value in making the things we need: understanding where they come from, how they are made, knowing what we can use to make them, and the confidence and enjoyment of these efforts. This connects us directly to the land and, if done in a community, to each other. It ties us to the place we inhabit and sets down roots.

Radical homemaking is not meant to be a paean to domesticity or a return to "traditional" gender roles (which are a relatively recent invention in many places). "Homemaking" should be understood here more broadly as the effort to make a home. This can mean building a house and caring for the house, but also building a community, getting in touch with the land and creating stories that give a sense of place. When understood in this sense, radical homemaking has goals and concerns very similar to those of bioregionalism.

8.5 CONCERNS ABOUT BIOREGIONALISM

Judith Plant agrees that bioregionalism is an attempt to "revalue home," but cautions we should make sure not to trap women in domesticity again.[4] Bioregionalism should thus be supplemented by a rigorous feminism.

Plant's concern reflects a broader issue with anarchism or the shift toward local democratic control: such control seems desirable, but we should be aware of how marginalized groups have been marginalized precisely through democratic control. For years in the US, "states' rights" have been marshaled to defend practices that are discriminatory yet democratically supported. LGBTQ folks, for example, have long faced discrimination from the majority.

While many environmentalists come from the left and would seek to prevent racism and other forms of discrimination, these tensions point to the unique political space that bioregionalism inhabits. The emphasis on small government has often been a position embraced by conservatives, while "big government" is commonly associated with regulations, including environmental regulations. Local governance is not necessarily in opposition to federal environmental regulations, but it does cut across current political trends in ways that can make for odd bedfellows. Radical homemaking, for example, attracts both ecologically focused leftists but also antigovernment conservatives.

8.6 EATING AND LIVING LOCALLY

While bioregionalism is more complicated than the injunction to eat and live local, this is certainly in the spirit of bioregionalism. Buying local, eating local, and living local keeps money within the community and supports local farms and businesses. Farmers' markets support local produce and feature food growing in season and in place. While eating and living locally alone will not fix the environmental crisis, it can function as a part of a bioregional practice that seeks to get in touch with place and community. It also points to the problem of food ethics that we will examine in the next chapter.

8.7 QUESTIONS FOR DISCUSSION

1. What is a bioregion? How does one bioregion differ from another? Why are bioregions relevant for environmentalism?
2. What does it mean to dwell in the land? What does it entail?
3. Why do some bioregionalists espouse anarchism? What do they mean by this?
4. What is radical homemaking?
5. What are some of the potential concerns about bioregionalism?

8.8 FURTHER READING

Kirkpatrick Sale has been a prominent advocate of bioregionalism; see his *Dwellers in the Land*. Judith Plant edited *Home! A Bioregional Reader*, although it is somewhat difficult to find. Michael Vincent McGinnis has also edited a more recent collection entitled *Bioregionalism*.

NOTES

1 Matthews, Freya. "Becoming Native: An Ethos of Countermodernity II." *Worldviews: Environment, Culture, Religion*, vol. 3, no. 3 (1999), 243–72.

2 Dodge, Jim. "Living by Life: Some Bioregional Theory and Practice." In Andruss, Plant et al., eds., *A Bioregional Reader* (Gabriola, BC: New Society Publishers, 1990), 5–12.

3 Sale, Kirkpatrick. *Dwellers in the Land: A Bioregional Vision* (Athens, GA: University of Georgia Press, 2000).

4 Plant, Judith. "Feminism and Bioregionalism." In Andruss, Plant et al., eds., *A Bioregional Reader* (Gabriola, BC: New Society Publishers, 1990), 21–23.

SECTION THREE

ENVIRONMENTAL MOVEMENTS

This section presents three environmental movements: Food Ethics, Animal Liberation and Mass Extinction, and Climate Change. What makes one set of debates and practices a "theory" and another a "movement" is not always clear. Ostensibly "theory" is being debated in academic journals and conferences, while "movements" are occurring out on the streets, although many theories can have an activist side while a movement might have a strong theoretical background. The animal liberation movement certainly has clear theoretical roots. Why split up theory and movements then?

Even though the theories in the last section and the movements in this section blur these boundaries, it is worth preserving the distinction between theory and practice (or movements) to maintain the tension between them. Environmentalism has always been more activist than typical philosophy, and preserving this distinction has the pedagogical function of reminding us that we need to do both: think through what we are doing and act.

Chapter 9 looks at food ethics. This is a relatively new academic field but one that is clearly of deep, real-world import. What we buy in a grocery store and what we eat may seem like mere matters of preference—but it affects people, animals, and ecosystems worldwide. Eating beef, for example, is one of the least environmentally friendly actions we can take. Beef is extremely inefficient, and it requires surprising amounts of water, feed, and land (to grow the feed) to raise cattle. Sadly, forests around the world are cut down to create the space needed to raise cattle and the food they eat. Altering what we eat and consumer demand for beef could have a profound effect on these issues.

Chapter 10 looks at the animal liberation movement and the current mass extinction. These topics are not directly related except in their shared concern with animals and animal suffering.

Chapter 11 is an overview of the environmental movement itself and its current primary incarnation as the climate change movement. Over time, shifts in environmentalism have reflected how environmental issues are articulated in public debate. This chapter traces some of these shifts and examines the significance of how we articulate various crises such as "climate change."

9

FOOD ETHICS

The last 20 years have seen the rise in both academic circles and in the public of concerns about the ethics of food. There are now textbooks and courses devoted to exactly this topic. Obviously, will not be able to cover the many aspects of food ethics in a single chapter, so our goal will be to discuss some examples of the kinds of topics covered in food ethics.

9.1 VEGETARIANISM

Environmentalists have long been concerned with the issue of meat consumption. The primary reason is the suffering to animals; we will examine this in the next chapter. A second reason is environmental damage. The list of environmental problems caused by the meat industry is well documented and long:

- toxic chemical residues in the food chain
- pharmaceutical additives in animal feeds
- polluting chemicals and animal waste from feedlot runoff in waterways and underground aquifers
- loss of topsoil caused by patterns of relentless grazing
- domestic and foreign deforestation and desertification resulting from the clearing of land for grazing and cultivating animal feed
- threatened habitats of wild species of plants and animals
- intensive exploitation of water and energy supplies
- ozone depletion caused by extensive use of fossil fuels and significant production of methane gas by cattle[1]

In short, the production of animal meat—beef in particular—is highly inefficient. Sitting down to eat a hamburger may feel innocuous, but it takes a surprising amount of resources to produce beef. Not only do cattle produce a lot of waste, but they drink a lot of water and eat a lot of feed, which itself requires lots of water and space. A "quarter pound of hamburger" requires "11,000L (2,904 gal) of water" and "each kilogram of 'edible beef' produces 40 kg (88 lb) of manure."[2] Every year more and more forests are cleared to make room for cattle and the production of food for cattle. Many of these forests are tropical rainforests comprising the highest amounts of biodiversity of any ecosystem. Slashing and burning these forests to make way for the production of hamburgers and steaks represents a critical decrease in biodiversity.

Becoming a vegetarian or a vegan, then, is not just a matter of decreasing the suffering of animals (more on this in the next chapter), but is also related to all the environmental damage done to produce meat. Thus, while it might not seem obvious at first, one might become a vegetarian out of concern for biodiversity.

The question of vegetarianism is complicated by issues of cultural and gender identity. Eating meat in some cultures has become associated with masculinity and is tied to masculine identity.[3] Women are sometimes associated with vegetables. Thus meat is often given primarily to men, and some men will even avoid eating vegetables because of their association with women. Furthermore, both Fox and Adams argue that a masculine identity with regards to meat is often associated with the domination of nature by men. Eating meat is a matter of masculine strength and prowess. For Adams, this domination of nature extends to women. A real man doesn't only dominate nature and eat meat, but he dominates women and has his way with them. She points to the ways that meat is sexualized and women treated like meat.

Not surprisingly then, for men who think this way, vegetarianism is offensively feminine. This creates an apathetic and frustrating situation in which arguing for vegetarianism is taken as an affront to masculine identity. But it is precisely this strutting, nature-domineering mentality that Fox thinks we need to overcome. In other words, becoming a vegetarian is a conscious decision to reject this domineering toxic masculinity.

Adams astutely recognizes that language is particularly important when it comes to comes meat. "Meat eaters ... [attempt] to impose a positive interpretation of what they know to be a tragedy (the tragedy of killing animals), but which they see as a necessary tragedy. They do so by manipulating language and meaning, creating a story that subjugates animal lives to human needs."[4] The grocery store doesn't sell "dead animals": it sells meat. We don't eat "charred cow flesh": we eat BBQ. For Adams, we see that there is thus a tacit acknowledgment in the standardized trivializations in our language about meat. That a vegetarian using language that disrupts these platitudes will make many uncomfortable and others mad is an indication the suffering of animals is indeed latently understood but consistently covered over. For Adams, this means that a vegetarian will always be something of a disruption in the status quo, even if she is not aggressively seeking to create one.

9.2 THE INDUSTRIALIZATION OF EATING

Industrialization and the invention of the assembly line have enabled massive increases in the production of food and commodities. At first blush, this would seem to be clearly good: more food means less hunger and starvation. But as Michael Pollan argues, there are worrisome side effects to the "industrialization of eating."[5] The key to Pollan's argument is that humans have coevolved with certain kinds of foods. It is important to notice that while humans have bred animals and plants to be useful for us, many of these relationships have also been helpful for the animals and plants involved. Thus, when humans cultivate rice, it may seem that humans are the ones profiting, but rice also profits and spreads from this relationship. The same is true for cattle. These food relationships require evolutionary adaptations from all involved. Humans, for example, had to evolve to become lactose tolerant to drink cow milk (some humans do not make enough lactose and get sick if they consume milk). Some wolves, on the other hand, have bred into dogs. Similarly, various plants have been spread far and wide thanks to human cultivation.

Pollan argues that these mutual relationships have evolved over hundreds and even thousands of years. But the industrialization of food has radically disrupted the kinds of foods we eat in ways that we do not fully understand and that can have damaging effects on human health. Pollan singles out five ways this has changed our diets.

"From Whole Foods to Refined Foods": The industrialization of food and the rise of food science have often sought to break foods into parts. Pollan gives the example of flour, which traditionally was ground into powder with the entire grain. This included the germ, which is the part of the grain containing nutrient-rich oils. But these oils are also what make flour go rancid with time. So, removing the germ produced white flour, which would go bad less quickly and therefore could be shipped more widely. This white flour was a prestige good at first, but it also produced less nutritious bread. Pollan claims that this led to epidemics of pellagra and beriberi because of the lack of vitamin B. Later, when the deficiencies of white flour were better understood, food scientists tried to add vitamin B back into the flour, but Pollan argues that isolating the parts in this way does not do justice to the whole. Other micronutrients are also missing, and we can't force them back into what they once were. In other words, Pollan's claim here is that scientifically designed refined foods are not the same as whole foods, and that we should be concerned about what may be lost in refined foods.

"From Complexity to Simplicity": This breaking down of whole foods into parts has also led to a less diverse diet. This may come as a surprise considering the great diversity of foods we find in grocery stores, but many of these foods are now scientifically created from a limited set of refined foods. The most famous example of this is high-fructose corn syrup, which is in seemingly everything. But the industrialization of food has also led to a simplification of the soils we use to grow plants and to the reduction of diversity among the kinds of plants we grow. We increasingly grow certain breeds of plants that produce the biggest, most efficient kinds of products we want, but this means a decrease in the diversity of the kinds of these plants we might eat and in the variations of nutrients that come from them. Instead of a variety of tomatoes, we might only eat the variety that is the biggest and reddest. Overall, the effect of these changes is simpler, more streamlined foods.

"From Quality to Quantity": The homogenization of food and soil decreases the food's quality in favor of quantity. This often means that we have to eat more to get the same amount of nutrients.

"From Leaves to Seeds": Since seeds are easier to store and ship, we eat more seeds than we used to and fewer leaves. This also represents a fundamental change in nutrients, which Pollan claims we don't yet fully understand.

"From Food Culture to Food Science": Lastly, food has traditionally been tied to culture and place. People ate food seasonally and in a unique and meaningful cultural and moral context that made food more than just food. Pollan worries that the industrialization of food takes food out of this cultural and moral context and turns it into abstract, largely meaningless consumables. In many senses of the word, this makes food something "empty." This emptiness of industrial food is seen in the complete disconnection of consumers from the products they buy. Most people simply do not see the grocery store as a morally fraught space. This empties the act of eating of the ethical and social import it always had before the industrialization of food.

On Pollan's account, the industrialization of food leads to a worrying impoverishment of our food, our food relationships, and our understanding of the moral and social implications of eating. He argues that we need to think about what we are eating and seek to eat locally and more ethically.

9.3 FARMING AND LABOR

Pollan is not alone in having these concerns. While his focus is on our alienated food diet, other environmentalists have focused on alienated and exploited labor in farming. Let us look first at the value of labor and then at the problem of exploitation.

Writers Wendell Berry and Joel Salatin have been influential if controversial advocates of small-scale or family farming. In his *Bringing It to the Table*, Berry defends the family farm. Like Pollan, who speaks of the dismemberment of food, Berry speaks of the "industrial dismemberment of labor" that degrades the minds of laborers and the quality of their products, and brings about a loss of pride in work.[6] Just as the industrialization of food empties food of meaning and morality, the industrialization of labor empties work of meaning and morality such that no one wants to do it anymore: "people live for quitting time, for weekends, for vacations, and for retirement...this is explained, of course, by the dullness of work, by the loss of responsibility for, or credit for, or knowledge of the thing made."[7]

For Berry the family farm is a site of meaningful labor, where work is not just doing tasks but making things. Hence meaningful work is experienced as art and love, the joy of making something as opposed the drudgery of doing tasks. For so many in modern society, this has become incomprehensible because "our economy is increasingly abstract, increasingly a thing of paper, unable either to describe or to serve the real economy...[and] it is this increasingly false or fantastical economy that is invoked as a standard of national health and happiness by our political leaders."[8] This dismemberment of meaningful labor that Berry describes is what Marx famously described as alienated labor.[9] Basically, according to Marx, the workers in industrial factories performed menial tasks that helped create a product they had no control over. Workers alienated (made strangers) from the product of their labor and even from their own laboring body. This is exactly what Berry sees happening with most work in the modern world.

The family farm, according to Berry, can be a site of meaningful, moral work. The work carried out on such a farm, if done right, is not dismembered, alienated, or irksome. Rather, it can be experienced as a matter of art and making. Berry's critics claim his approach is impractical (are we all to buy family farms?) and romantic, but even they concede that this doesn't change the force of his critique of alienated labor.

This dismemberment of the economy results not only in the alienation of both work and worker, but, worse, in the exploitation of labor. Critics of industrial agriculture have long pointed to the ways that immigrant labor in particular is egregiously exploited. In a now-famous exposé, Barry Estabrook showed how immigrant workers in Immokalee, Florida were

subjected to beatings, locked in trucks, and coerced into "involuntary ser-
vitude"—in short, that in some cases their treatment amounted to slavery.[10]
Estabrook's journalism inspired the film *Food Chains*, which examines
the exploitation of immigrants in Florida and California.[11] In California,
exploitation has long occurred in the Central Valley and in places like Napa
Valley. The exploitative conditions in California were dramatically contested
by figures such as Dolores Huerta and Cesar Chavez in the 1960s and 1970s.
While conditions have improved, Estabrook and *Food Chains* make it clear
that exploitation is ongoing.

9.4 CAFOS

At the heart of these issues is an ethical battle. On the one side, we have the
claim that the efficiency of modern practices has massive positive consequences: we feed more people than ever before, and health and life expectancy have improved dramatically. On the other side, we have the claim that
there are critically dangerous problems related to these practices: yes, we
have more food, but it is not necessarily healthier, is unethically produced,
and has devastating environmental consequences.

Perhaps the best embodiment of this disagreement is CAFO, or "concentrated animal feed operation." These are industrial farms that raise at least
1,000 "animal units" in a single location. Opponents of CAFOs point to the
cramped and miserable condition of the animals, the resulting waste pollution,
and the inhumanity of the entire system. Supporters of CAFOs claim they are
efficient and produce more food than could be done otherwise in a smaller
space (sometimes this is even argued to be environmentally more efficient than
having the same number of animals spread out over a large space). CAFOs may
smell and look unpleasant, but the benefits are greater than the costs.

I bring this conflict up not to resolve it, but to illustrate the ethical tensions between the imperative of efficiency in modern food science and food
production and the concerns of animal welfare advocates and food ethics. It
is important to note that both sides are claiming to do something ethical: the
ethics of efficiency on the one hand and an ethical concern with inhumane
conditions and unethical disconnection (from the animals, workers, the
larger whole, etc.) on the other.

9.5 SLOW FOOD

As the arguments about food and farming in this chapter have shown,
many environmentalist thinkers push back against the modern morality of efficiency. Yes, small farms are not as efficient as CAFOs, but they

are more ethical. Yes, whole foods can be more expensive and harder to produce in quantity, but they are healthier and more ethically made. Yes, it may be difficult to be a vegetarian, but it is ethically more responsible to be one.

For many environmentalists, fast food is the embodiment of what is wrong with the modern ethics of efficiency. Fast food is unhealthy, unethically produced, unethically sourced, cheap, vulgar, wrapped in plastic, and ubiquitous. This change in our food reflects a larger change in modern society that George Ritzer famously calls the "McDonaldization of society."[12] Not surprisingly, one of the groups critical of these changes has called itself the slow movement and, with regard to food, the slow food movement. Slow food refers not just to how food is produced, but to the love and care that go into making it and eating it. According to the Carl Honoré,

> Fast and Slow do more than just describe a rate of change. They are shorthand for ways of being, or philosophies of life. Fast is busy, controlling, aggressive, hurried, analytical, stressed, superficial, impatient, active, quantity-over-quality. Slow is the opposite: calm, careful, receptive, still, intuitive, unhurried, patient, reflective, quality-over-quantity. It is about making real and meaningful connections—with people, culture, work, food, everything. The paradox is that Slow does not always mean slow. As we shall see, performing a task in a Slow manner often yields faster results. It is also possible to do things quickly while maintaining a Slow frame of mind.[13]

The slow food movement is a call to be mindful about what we eat, as opposed to the thoughtlessness of fast-food culture.

9.6 INTERSECTIONALITY AND FOOD

The ethics of where food comes from, how it is produced, and how we relate to it must be intersectional. This is to say, it must pay attention to the position of food in a complex nexus of race, gender, culture, class, etc. Take class, for example. Recent discussions of "vegan privilege" have drawn attention to the ways in which ethical food is often expensive. Whether local, organic, slow, vegetarian, or vegan, ethically-produced food is often more expensive than cheap mass-produced goods. The result is a tiered food system. For those who live in "food deserts," where the only food that is available may be fast food and cheap grocery goods, eating healthy and ethically may not be possible or may be extremely difficult. Some simply might not be able to afford more ethically produced food. As such, eating local, organic, slow, vegetarian, or vegan can be a privilege and also function as a sign of privilege: eating more ethically is possible—if you can pay for it. The bizarre result is that some may buy more ethically-produced food not for ethical reasons but to feel or signal being rich. Meanwhile, those who can't afford to buy expensive or healthier foods may be shamed for eating unethical foods or for suffering the effects of eating unhealthy food (such as weight gain). Understandably, this can create resentment toward those who insist everyone should eat more ethically or be vegans or vegetarians.

That some humans only have access to some food options should alert us to the ways in which food can be colonial or imperialistic. Cheap, Americanized food is flooding the world, ostensibly alleviating hunger but also eliminating traditional cultural food practices. Many Native Americans in the US are currently fighting for Indigenous food sovereignty. Here the Indigenous struggle for the right to control one's own destiny (tribal sovereignty) is applied to food, and attention is drawn to the ways in which mass-produced food inevitably alters culture. The US highly subsidizes American farmers, and this allows for cheap exports that undermine other markets. Why produce rice via traditional (slow) means, when one can buy it cheaply from another country? In purely economic terms, this seems like a rational choice. But this sidelines how cultures and traditional livelihoods are deeply intertwined with food. As many scholars have shown, the green revolution in India (the introduction of Western agricultural practices) caused widespread disruptions for many people, especially rural women. Native Americans seeking to preserve and protect their traditions have found that they have to push back against mass-produced foods and reassert traditional practices.

These are just some examples that illustrate the far-reaching interconnections of food, culture, race, gender, class, etc. Very little is more important and more fraught than our food.

9.7 QUESTIONS FOR DISCUSSION
1. Vegetarianism is often about preventing animal suffering, but it can also be about the environment. How so?
2. Why might we worry about the industrialization of eating?
3. Why does where our food comes from matter?
4. What is the moral impulse behind efficiency?
5. Why might someone want to be inefficient?

9.8 FURTHER READING

For more on vegetarianism, see Carol Adams's *The Sexual Politics of Meat*. Michael Pollan's *Omnivore's Dilemma* and *In Defense of Food* were both successful books. Wendell Berry is also a prolific author of many books about farming. Lastly, Carl Honoré's *In Praise of Slowness* is the classic work of the slow movement. Winona LaDuke's *Recovering the Sacred* includes examples of efforts by Native Americans to defend their traditional practices and foods.

Notes

1 Fox, Michael Allen. "Vegetarianism and Treading Lightly on the Earth." In Pojman, Louis P. et al., eds., *Environmental Ethics: Readings in Theory and Application* (Boston, MA: Wadsworth Publishing, 2016), 533–41.

2 Ibid.

3 Adams, Carol J. *The Sexual Politics of Meat: A Feminist-Vegetarian Critical Theory* (New York: Bloomsbury, 2015).

4 Ibid., 78.

5 Pollan, Michael. *In Defense of Food: An Eater's Manifesto* (New York: Penguin, 2009).

6 Berry, Wendell. *Bring It to the Table: On Farming and Food* (Berkeley, CA: Counterpoint, 2009), 35.

7 Ibid.

8 Ibid., 37.

9 Tucker, Robert C., ed. *The Marx–Engels Reader.* (New York: W.W. Norton, 1978).

10 Estabrook, Barry. "Politics of the Plate: The Price of Tomatoes." *Gourmet*, March 2009.

11 Rawal, Sanjay. *Food Chains* [Film]. (2014).

12 Ritzer, George. *The McDonaldization of Society* (Los Angeles, CA: SAGE, 2013).

13 Honoré, Carl. *In Praise of Slowness: Challenging the Cult of Speed* (New York: Harper One, 2005), 14–15.

10

ANIMAL LIBERATION AND MASS EXTINCTION

This chapter deals with two distinct threats to animals. The first concerns the way animals are exploited and suffer due to human use and abuse. The second examines human-caused mass extinction. While the former is a result of speciesism—the idea that humans are superior to animals—the latter is an accident.

10.1 ANIMAL LIBERATION

In 1975 Peter Singer published *Animal Liberation*, a book he hoped would change human-animal relations. It appeared at a time when the very definition of what it means to be human was being debated, especially in light of the 1973 *Roe v. Wade* decision in the US. Conservative opponents of abortion who were looking to define the fetus as fully human were seeking for nonreligious criteria. John Noonan had argued that what makes us human is our genetic code, which we have at fertilization.[1] The fetus, then, at any stage of pregnancy, is fully human, and aborting it is murder.

Defenders of the right to abortion opposed such claims. Mary Anne Warren argued that definitions like Noonan's equivocated on what it means to be human.[2] She claimed that Noonan was giving a biological definition of what it means to be human, when rights are based not merely on biology but on social and moral "personhood." She asked how we would know if an alien being we discovered was like a human or more like a cow. To be like a human would require certain features, such as 1. "consciousness" (including the ability to feel pain), 2. "reasoning," 3. "self-motivated activity," 4. "the capacity to communicate," and 5. "the presence of self-concepts" and self-awareness.[3] For Warren, the fetus did not have these capabilities and thus wasn't fully human until birth. Critics worried that infants and people with certain disabilities did not have these features and thus on this definition of personhood could not be considered people. For our purposes, we need not delve into each of these features in detail or into further details of this debate. Rather, what interests us is that some animals *do* manifest these features and thus, according to these criteria, have personhood.

We now know that there are actually many animals that manifest some or all of these features: dolphins, pigs, higher apes, some birds, and others. If this is the case, should these animals be given personhood? Should we stop eating them? In 2018 in Oregon, a judge threw out a lawsuit filed on behalf of a horse against a former owner who had neglected and abused it. The judge made the following statement:

> The court grants with prejudice defendant's motion to dismiss based on a lack of standing for Justice the horse. The court finds that a non-human animal such as Justice lacks the legal status or qualifications necessary for the assertion of legal rights and duties in a court of law....
>
> There are profound implications of a judicial finding that a horse, or any non-human animal for that matter, is a legal entity that has the legal right to assert a claim in a court of law. Such a finding would likely lead to a flood of lawsuits whereby non-human animals could assert claims we now reserve just for humans and human creations such as business and other entities.[4]

This may be exactly the sort of thing the animal liberation movement would want to see occur and indicates, from this perspective, how contemporary human existence is built on the systematic exploitation of animals. Treating animals as equal to humans would completely undermine the economics and social structures of modern life. (Note that businesses can count as persons, but animals cannot.)

Questioning the obviousness of the superiority of humans is precisely what Singer set out to do in *Animal Liberation*. Singer based his argument on utilitarianism, the most prominent modern ethical theory. Utilitarianism claims that we should seek to produce the greatest amount of good for the greatest number of people, or stated negatively, decrease as much suffering as we can for the most people possible. Singer points out that we have no reason to think that the suffering of many animals is dissimilar to our own. As such, if we are committed to decreasing suffering, our efforts should encompass both human suffering and nonhuman animal suffering.

There are two things to notice here. First, Singer questions the sacred or special status of humans. He calls this speciesism.[5] Second, by focusing on suffering Singer is moving the debate away from rights. The question for Singer is not What rights do animals have? but Do they suffer?

How do we decrease the suffering of animals? Most obviously, stop eating them. But, in terms of suffering, eating animals is not the primary problem, but rather the cruel conditions under which many of these animals are raised. Chickens that have a comfortable life and are cared for will suffer some pain when killed, granted, but industrialized meat production conditions for animals are cruel and inhumane. Pigs and chickens are often raised in tiny cages, injected with hormones, and shut in the dark. Such animals become mere objects to be used as industries see fit to maximize their profits. It is no surprise that meat processing centers have sophisticated security systems and are highly sensitive about being filmed.

When we go into the grocery store or eat at a restaurant, we don't see this suffering. We don't see where the food comes from, how it was raised, who picked or killed it, how it was killed, how it got here, how long it was refrigerated, who prepared it, how much they were paid—the exploitation and suffering involved are hidden. As such, if we are committed to decreasing suffering, we also need to seek to make it transparent by extricating it from the many forces that want to hide it. This is both a social and an individual task, as there are many ways we can be oblivious to what is unpleasant. Singer famously pointed out that everyday consumer choices are fraught with these tensions. He asks us to imagine the following scenario. We have just bought a new pair of shoes and are walking outside when we see a small child sinking in a pool of water. There is no time to think: if we want to save this child, we will have to jump in after it immediately, even in our new shoes. Singer believes that it should be obvious that not to jump in in order to spare our new shoes is clearly unethical. But around the world, children are suffering and are at risk from diseases. While they might not be dying in front of us, the decision to spend $100 on a pair of shoes is a decision not to send that money to help dying children.

Humans will go to great lengths to hide from themselves the suffering and exploitations of animals and humans that make many of our modern comforts possible. The animal liberation movement that was inspired by Singer has sought to make the suffering of animals visible and to undermine the justifications for such suffering, especially the speciesist claim that humans are superior to nonhuman animals. Nonetheless, some environmental philosophers continue to have fundamental concerns about animal liberation.

10.2 ANIMAL LIBERATION VS. ENVIRONMENTAL ETHICS

Animal liberation did not always receive a warm welcome from environmental philosophers. Both deep ecology and ecocentrism push for a holistic understanding of environmental issues. This privileges the whole over the parts. Thus, if an invasive species is disrupting an ecosystem, believers in these approaches have no qualms about systematically eliminating it. From the perspective of a consistent animal liberation approach, such behavior could be viewed as unethical if it causes pain and suffering. But the holistic approaches point out that there is always pain and suffering inherent in ecosystems. Wolves and tigers eat deer, and they aren't always nice about it. The point is not that these approaches are callous toward pain, but that they consider pain an inevitable part of healthy ecosystems. Thus, there seems to be a fundamental difference between animal liberation and ecology regarding animal suffering.

But there is also a deeper philosophical difference at stake. Environmental philosophy has almost always been deeply critical of modernity and, as we have seen, often sought the sources of the environmental crisis in the philosophical underpinnings of modernity. Environmental philosophers often treat the utilitarian approach of modernity with scorn precisely because of the ways it has been used to justify human domination in modernity. Thus, when Singer sought to use utilitarianism to liberate animals, some felt it was an effort to use an oppressive logic to fix an oppressive logic. Singer then seemed to be working from within modernity to fix modernity in exactly the way that deep ecology deemed shallow.

Between the seeming rejection of the holistic approach of much of environmental philosophy and the "shallow" marshaling of the utilitarian logic of modernity, animal liberation has been, and even today continues to be, viewed with suspicion by some environmental philosophers. With that said, there is no question that the animal liberation movement has been influential and has played an active role in raising awareness about the suffering of animals in industrial meat production and in encouraging more sustainable diet and consumption practices.

10.3 ANIMAL LIBERATION VS. ANIMAL RIGHTS

While the utilitarian approach of animal liberation did not sit well with environmental philosophers that took their bearings from ecology, it was also challenged by a position known as animal rights. *The Case for Animal Rights* by Tom Regan made a philosophical case similar to Singer's in *Animal Liberation*: it expanded a traditional ethical theory—in this case Kantian deontology—to include animals.[6] But Singer's utilitarian approach and

Regan's Kantian approach had different implications. While Singer focused on animal suffering, Regan and the animal rights movement focused on the inherent dignity of animals and sought to extend to animals the kinds of rights normally afforded humans alone. In practice, this led to a stronger stance against using animals for human purposes. These objections were often articulated in terms of interests: the animal rights position is that human interests should not override animal interests and that animals should not be subject to human violence. Singer's utilitarian approach, which is now commonly referred to as "animal welfare," focuses on decreasing the suffering of animals but does allow for their humane use by humans.

Animal welfare/liberation and animal rights adherents, therefore, disagree fundamentally about the human use of animals, but they do agree that the broader, ecological approach of environmental philosophy is often too focused on biodiversity and extinction in terms of environmental policy. Animal welfare and animal rights advocates are more likely to be found protesting against factories and raising awareness about the condition of animals used for food, whereas ecologically focused environmentalists are more likely to be found protesting against global warming, mass extinction, and deforestation.

10.4 THE SIXTH MASS EXTINCTION

The second topic of this chapter is not connected to the first except insofar as they both concern nonhuman animals. While animal liberation is concerned primarily with animals used for food, mass extinction concerns the die-off of species worldwide.

In 2018 a major report from the World Wildlife Fund claimed that "humanity has wiped out 60% of mammals, birds, fish, and reptiles since 1970."[7] Rivers and other freshwater habitats have been particularly hard hit, with an 83% collapse in populations. The environmental scientist Bob Watson argues that "Nature contributes to human wellbeing culturally and spiritually, as well as through the critical production of food, clean water, and energy, and through regulating the Earth's climate, pollution, pollination, and floods. The Living Planet report clearly demonstrates that human activities are destroying nature at an unacceptable rate, threatening the wellbeing of current and future generations."[8] According to that report, the primary culprits are the clearing of land for farms and hunting.

In 2019, a "global scientific review" of insect populations showed that "More than 40% of insect species are declining and a third are endangered... The rate of extinction is eight times faster than that of mammals, birds, and reptiles. The total mass of insects is falling by a precipitous 2.5%

a year, according to the best data available, suggesting they could vanish within a century."[9] Insects are of course integral to the survival of all ecosystems.

Amphibians are at particularly high risk. The UN reports that 40% of amphibian species are in danger of extinction.[10] Some places are witnessing bird die-offs.[11] Many of the world's iconic species, such as giraffes, cheetahs, rhinos, elephants, and tigers, are at risk.

According to Elizabeth Kolbert, we are in the midst of a sixth mass extinction.[12] In the history of the Earth, there have been five mass extinctions, but the current one is the only one caused by humans.

The sixth mass extinction is a crisis in need of a movement. In light of the stunning scale and tragedy of our situation, it is astounding that this crisis fails to be at the forefront of the public eye. That it is not evinces not only of our continued anthropocentrism and economism, but is also a reflection of the sheer amount of noise and purposeful deception in the media. Why such a critical event and more broadly the global climate crisis have not been adequately addressed will be the topic of this book's last section.

One aspect of this crisis is worth flagging: a sixth mass extinction would be an accident. Humans have not set out to systematically destroy animal species. We may be anthropocentric, we may be caught up in an ever-accelerating world economy, but this mass extinction, including potentially our own extinction, is not the result of maliciousness: it is an unintended consequence. However, the fact that it is unwilled makes it harder for us to take responsibility for it. We feel less perturbed about manslaughter than murder. Oddly, then, the lack of intention worsens the crisis. There is no 'bad guy'. There is just us caught up in machinery we don't fully understand, with effects we didn't intend. Nonetheless, we need to take responsibility. The last section of this text examines the various forces that have hindered us from doing so.

Before turning to that section, however, I want to take stock of the environmental movement, discuss how it has changed over time and how it is currently being articulated. This is the topic of the next chapter.

10.5 QUESTIONS FOR DISCUSSION
1. What is the animal liberation movement? What is it seeking and why?
2. What is speciesism?
3. How did Singer use utilitarianism to make his argument and why does this run afoul of some environmental philosophers?
4. What is the sixth extinction? What is the significance of it being an accident?

10.6 FURTHER READING

Peter Singer's *Animal Liberation* is the key text of the animal liberation movement and is still very influential today. Elizabeth Kolbert won the Pulitzer Prize for her work *The Sixth Extinction*.

Notes

1 Noonan Jr., John T. *The Morality of Abortion: Legal and Historical Perspectives* (Cambridge, MA: Harvard University Press, 1970).

2 Warren, Mary Anne. "On the Moral and Legal Status of Abortion." *The Monist*, vol. 57, no. 1 (1973), 43–61.

3 Ibid.

4 Osborne, Mark. "Judge throws out lawsuit filed by horse against former owner." *Yahoo! News*, 18 September, 2018.

5 Speciesism: the belief that humans are better than nonhuman animals.

6 Regan, Tom. *The Case for Animal Rights* (Berkeley, CA: University of California Press, 2004).

7 Carrington, Damian. "Humanity has wiped out 60% of animal populations since 1970, report finds." *The Guardian*, 30 October, 2018.

8 Ibid.

9 Carrington, Damian. "Plummeting insect numbers 'threaten collapse of nature'." *The Guardian*, 10 February, 2019.

10 Woodward, Aylin. "Frogs are dying off at record rates—an ominous sign the 6th mass extinction is hitting one group of creatures hardest." *Business Insider*, 7 June, 2019.

11 Johnson, Kevin. "The Southwest Is Facing an 'Unprecedented' Migratory Bird Die-Off." *Audubon*, 16 September, 2020.

12 Kolbert, Elizabeth. *The Sixth Extinction: An Unnatural History* (New York: Henry Holt and Co., 2014).

11

THE CLIMATE CHANGE MOVEMENT

Like any movement, the environmental movement has changed with time and championed different points of emphasis over its history. While we lack the space to provide a full history here, the goal of this chapter is to give a brief outline of the environmental movement and examine the significance of the rise of climate change as the fundamental issue in environmentalism.

11.1 ANTECEDENTS TO THE ENVIRONMENTAL MOVEMENT

There are many figures, movements, and ideas that predate the modern environmental movement that remain influential for environmentalists today. There is a long history of humans defending the commons, or public lands that are accessible to all, from enclosure and appropriation.[1] This could be peasants in early modern England, Native Americans both past and present, and rural farmers in Africa, Asia, and the Americas right now. While we do not always have clear records of exactly what these people said or did to fight back, in many places their efforts have left an imprint on cultural memory: the image of the people fighting for their common land. Historical Native American figures, many of whom protested against colonial practices and spoke out in defense of their land, have become influential among today's environmentalists.

Other figures and movements are still read about today but often have an ambivalent status. Take Romanticism, for example: a movement of the late 1700s and early 1800s that was responding to the Enlightenment and the beginnings of industrialization. Unlike Enlightenment thinkers, who tended to emphasize science, rationality, and modern progress, the Romantics criticized the dehumanizing effects of industrialism, the modern denigration of the past, and the overconfidence in rationality. Importantly for our focus here, they found poetic inspiration in nature. In fact, they are often accused of romanticizing both nature itself and Indigenous peoples, turning the latter into facile caricatures that could be marshaled as foils to modernity. In short, the Romantic movement was an attempted inversion of the value of modern civilization over nature, wilderness, and non-modern peoples.

The mid-1800s saw various important writers valorizing nature. Works by the American Transcendentalists are still read today, including the essays of Ralph Waldo Emerson, Henry David Thoreau's *Walden*, and Walt Whitman's *Leaves of Grass*. Then the late 1800s saw the rise of various conservation efforts, including the creation of John Muir's Sierra Club in 1892. Muir helped establish National Parks in the US. In the early 1900s, forester Gifford Pinchot and Theodore Roosevelt also sought to conserve forests. The first ecological journals appeared around this time and influenced conservationist Aldo Leopold.

Again, throughout these years, humans all over the world protested the enclosure of the commons and the privatization of land. However, the various environmentally focused writings and efforts prior to the modern environmental movement tend to be fragmented, and while they did have some (mostly small) effects on political policy, I will not attempt to trace those effects here. Generally speaking, however, environmentalism as a modern movement is thought to have begun with the social and cultural revolutions of the 1960s and 1970s.

11.2 THE ENVIRONMENTAL MOVEMENT

The beginning of the environmental movement is often attributed to Rachel Carson's *Silent Spring*, published in 1962. While often remembered for raising awareness of the infamous pesticide DDT, "'Silent Spring' was more than a study of the effects of synthetic pesticides; it was an indictment of the late 1950s. Humans, Carson argued, should not seek to dominate nature through chemistry, in the name of progress. In Carson's view, technological innovation could easily and irrevocably disrupt the natural system."[2]

Silent Spring not only defended an ecological approach but did so in a way that caught the public's eye. It also helped that it was written at the beginning of the cultural revolutions of the 1960s, including the civil rights movement, gay rights movement, counterculture, and hippy movements. This was a period of foment and interest in radical alternatives that also saw the rise of the scientific discipline of ecology and of the animal liberation movement. Historically, the early 1970s was a particularly important time for environmental philosophy, as many influential theoretical approaches and foundational environmental philosophers can be traced to this period, which was followed by the rapid proliferation of environmental debates, writings, and movements.

Different concerns have been prominent at different points during the environmental movement, including pollution, animal rights, animal liberation, rain forest destruction, acid rain, the ozone hole, global warming, decreasing diversity, among others. Currently, the primary focus of the environmental movement is climate change. What is climate change and why has it recently become the face of the environmental movement?

11.3 CLIMATE CHANGE

What exactly is climate change? Although the basic facts are clear, I am not going to present data here to try and prove this.[3] This is not because such data are hard to find, but because, as we will see in the next chapter, climate deniers reject any scientific consensus on the issue. They claim we must keep debating it and maintain the status quo for now. However, there is scientific consensus and now is not the time to debate whether climate change is real or not. Now is the time for action.

Climate change involves human-caused massive increases in greenhouse gases like carbon dioxide and methane, which trap heat on the Earth and generate global warming. Increasing temperatures can lead to many things, including increasingly volatile weather patterns, overall warmer weather that can lead to more wildfires, disruption of ecosystems, extinction of species, and melting of glaciers, with the ensuing rise in sea levels. This last point in particular has dire consequences for humans because if the polar ice caps were to melt, the rising oceans would flood our densely populated coastal cities. This would lead to mass human migration and cause disastrous economic damage.

Notice how the imagery evoked in the last sentence is focused on the effects on humans and the economy. One of the reasons climate change has proven a powerful face for environmentalism is because it can appeal directly to the anthropocentric and economic concerns of modern humankind. Unfortunately, as we have seen in the first section of this book, modernity is thoroughly anthropocentric. As we will see in Chapter 14, it has also come increasingly under the sway of economism—the idea that the economy and economic growth is a fundamental human and political concern. Thus, although we are witnessing a catastrophic human-caused sixth mass extinction, it is difficult to get people to care. But the image of the destruction of coastal cities, the radical disruption of human economies, and the displacement of millions of people garners far more attention.

While it is unfortunate that our institutional priorities tend to put the economy first, human wellbeing second, and the wellbeing of nonhumans last, climate change effects all of these. Climate change is thus something of a catch-all. Addressing climate change will not fix mass extinction as effectively as addressing mass extinction directly, but as it is far easier to get humans to care about climate change, addressing it would help raise awareness of some of the issues of mass extinction. In other words, environmentalists of different stripes would likely agree that we should do something about climate change.

We have just seen in the last chapter that proponents of the animal liberation movement didn't always get along with ecologically oriented environmentalists. They differ fundamentally about what exactly we should be doing. Regardless of these differences, however, both camps are likely to agree that we need to address climate change.

Climate change, then, has the virtue of reaching across environmental aisles and across anthropocentric and economy-oriented boundaries; as such, it can collect a coalition of advocates that might usually disagree. It also transcends national boundaries. One of the most vocal climate change advocates is Greta Thunberg, a young Swedish activist who has directly challenged world leaders in various forums. Since climate change is a global phenomenon, it will require global coordination to address it. And indeed, various efforts have been made to establish global standards to reduce greenhouse gas emissions, such as the 2015 International Paris Agreement.

Furthermore, climate change forces us to pay attention to other details, such as environmental racism, the concept that the brunt of climate change and pollution often falls on disadvantaged racial groups or countries. It will not simply be enough for rich countries to decrease emissions, as impoverished countries are often in a worse position to combat emissions (as well as deforestation, water contamination, etc.).

So, climate change is a complicated, multipronged problem that requires international research, coordination, and institutional changes. No one country will solve it on its own, which is why we have international research in the form of the Intergovernmental Panel on Climate Change, established in 1988, which regularly publishes the results of international scientific consensus and suggestions for government policy changes. By 1995, the IPCC had recognized the effect of human activities on climate change. By 2001, they were arguing that the evidence was even stronger and in 2007 they called it "unequivocal."[4]

Almost every day we can read about scientists being shocked by the speed of climate change and by the mass species die-off going on all around us. And yet very little seems to change. Why? Why, if there is scientific consensus, is there so little institutional action?

This is the alarming question addressed in this book's last section, which will begin with the disturbing problem of climate denial.

11.4 GETTING INVOLVED

While climate change is arguably the overarching concern of the environmental movement, there are so many complexities and so many interrelated issues that it is perhaps better to speak of environmental movements. If you would like to get involved, there are many organizations to choose from. Faye Lessler has created a helpful list, which I include below both to encourage you to find out more and to highlight the diversity of environmental movements:[5]

Social and Environmental Justice
1. Cultural Survival (amplify Indigenous voices and protect Indigenous peoples)
2. A Growing Culture (to help small farmers and farmer autonomy)
3. Native American Traditional Food Systems (regenerate Native American foodways)
4. Fashion Revolution (more ethical fashion industry)
5. Earthjustice (organization of environmental law)
6. School Girls Unite (fight prejudice against girls)
7. National Resource Defense Council (protect air, water, wilderness)

Conservation and Reforestation
8. One Percent for the Planet (encourages companies to donate to environmental causes)
9. American Forests (forest conservation)
10. Conservation International (protect land, oceans)
11. Eden Projects (reforestation)
12. One Tree Planted (reforestation)
13. WeForest (reforestation)
14. Rainforest Alliance (certify rainforest-friendly products)

Wildlife Protection
15. Jane Goodall Institute (wildlife conservation)
16. The National Audubon Society (protect birds)

17. Nature Conservancy (protect water and lands for wildlife)
18. Sierra Club (environmental advocacy)
19. Wildlife Conservation Society (protect natural habitats)
20. World Wildlife Fund (endangered species)

Ocean Conservation
21. 5 Gyres Institute (fight plastic pollution)
22. Blue Sphere Foundation (ocean conservation)
23. Lonely Whale Foundation (environmental business solutions)
24. Oceana (marine biodiversity)
25. SeaLegacy (visual storytelling concerning the ocean)

Climate Justice
26. 350.org (oppose coal and gas, support clean energy)
27. Cool Effect (reduce carbon emissions)
28. Earth Guardians (youth-led environmentalism)
29. Greenpeace (environmental activism)
30. Project Drawdown (education)

Ecological Agriculture
31. Fibershed (decentralized, local textile systems)
32. Regenerative Agriculture Alliance (food through Indigenous approaches)
33. Regeneration International (rebuild deteriorated ecological systems)
34. The Soil Association (sustainable food systems)
35. Sustainable Harvest International (sustainable farming)

11.5 QUESTIONS FOR DISCUSSION
1. What is climate change? What causes it?
2. Why has it proven to be a powerful rallying cry for environmentalism?
3. Why do you think there is still such reluctance to fix climate change?

11.6 FURTHER READING
The scientific consensus on climate change is widely available in the IPCC reports, which are available gratis online. The history of these reports is fascinating, as they trace how scientists became increasingly alarmed by the crisis.

Notes

1 Federici, Silvia. *Re-Enchanting the World: Feminism and the Politics of the Commons* (Oakland, CA: PM Press, 2018).

2 Griswold, Eliza. "How 'Silent Spring' Ignited the Environmental Movement." *New York Times Magazine*, 21 September, 2012.

3 If you want mountains of data, see the Intergovernmental Panel on Climate Change reports, available online.

4 Oreskes, Naomi and Erik M. Conway. *Merchants of Doubt: How a Handful of Scientists Obscured the Truth on Issues from Tobacco Smoke to Global Warming* (New York: Bloomsbury Press, 2011), 169.

5 This list is from https://greendreamer.com/journal/environmental-organizations-nonprofits-for-a-sustainable-future. Accessed 16 October, 2021. There are many such lists online. Although I cannot vouch for every organization on this list, I encourage you to use this list, other lists, and the websites of these organizations to obtain more information.

SECTION FOUR

WHY ARE WE NOT DOING MORE?

If the environmental crisis is indeed as desperate as scientists say it is, why is so little being done about it? This question is particularly important because the primary effort to promote change often seems to be raising awareness. In other words, often the assumption is that if more people correctly understood the precariousness of this situation, we would do something about it. However, that so little is being done suggests that many are still not fully aware of the dire nature of the situation, and so we must do more to raise that awareness. Thus we end up caught in a cycle of raising awareness.

This does not mean that we should not be raising awareness. Rather, it implies there are other factors in play that affect raising awareness and make it an extremely difficult or inadequate endeavor. The first is active and systematic deception on the part of financially and/or politically motivated agents. Some companies and political groups not only deny climate change and other environmental issues but seek to spread widespread doubt and foster ignorance about environmental science and the environmental crisis. Sometimes these efforts are clearly motivated simply by greed, while at others they are driven by complex cultural and political issues tied to identity and/or different visions of how society should be organized. While the desire for profit is overt, motivations tied to culture, ideology, or identity can often be covert, such that groups advocating for them might not even fully articulate or understand the position they are taking. Perhaps the most obvious example of this is anthropocentrism, which is widespread in modern society and rarely recognized. Many simply assume that humans are more important than nonhumans without ever thinking about why. Hence this section addresses both the overt and tacit forces that contribute to the failure to do more about the environmental crisis.

The first chapter in this section, Chapter 12, focuses on the overt forces behind climate denial. It relies on Naomi Oreskes and Erik Conway's important work, *Merchants of Doubt*.[1] In addition to showing that there are organizations actively sowing doubt about the reality of environmental crisis, the authors examine the reasons why some misguided scientists joined these efforts. Thus, Oreskes and Conway alert us not only to widespread deception, but also to the complex motives (beyond profit) that can inform such efforts.

Part of what is confounding about this situation is that good, intelligent people can be disturbingly ignorant and deluded when it comes to environmental issues. Chapter 13 seeks to help us understand this by looking at "epistemologies of ignorance." This rather new concept was introduced by Charles Mills to examine race and how ignorance about race is taught and established. In other words, for Mills, certain forms of ignorance comprise not a lack of learning but rather learned ignorance. With regard to the environment, much of the resistance to radical change is due to anti-environmentalist or anthropocentric indoctrination.

This learned ignorance is often built upon more fundamental assumptions, such as economism or myths and narratives about modern progress. These involve stories about what it is to be human or how humans have, do, and should relate to each other and to nonhumans. Chapter 14 examines these narratives and how they shape our ethical and unethical relationships with one another and the world.

Chapter 15 examines thoughtlessness. The claim in this chapter is that there are forces that actively discourage us not just from thinking about environmental issues, but from certain forms of thinking in general.

Lastly, Chapter 16 introduces the issue of world alienation and the problem of our disconnection with and lack of love for the Earth.

NOTE

1   Oreskes, Naomi and Erik M. Conway. *Merchants of Doubt: How a Handful of Scientists Obscured the Truth on Issues from Tobacco Smoke to Global Warming* (New York: Bloomsbury Press, 2011).

12

CLIMATE DENIAL

The last section of this book will explore how normal people involved in everyday activities can be contributing to great evil, including the current environmental crisis. This doesn't exculpate those involved but shows that dealing with the environmental crisis means recognizing that it is more complicated than good guys and bad guys. Good people can also do great damage. This chapter, however, seeks to show that there are indeed bad guys seeking to mislead and deceive us out of addressing global warming. Who would do such a thing and why?

To explore this issue, this chapter will look at Naomi Oreskes and Erik Conway's *Merchants of Doubt: How a Handful of Scientists Obscured the Truth on Issues from Tobacco Smoke to Global Warming*. This exposé outlines the methods and rationale behind efforts to deny climate change. While the next chapters show how many of us are complicit in environmental problems, this chapter will show how some are tricked and misled into climate denial, while political discourse is muddied to delay any needed changes. This chapter begins by outlining the issues attacked by these merchants of doubt, then examines their methods and their rationale for doing so.

12.1 THE ISSUES

Oreskes and Conway (hereafter O&C) document the development of a series of methods that are now being marshaled to obscure the reality of climate change. The primary villains of this story are Fred Singer and Fred Seitz who, along with a "handful of other scientists...joined forces with think tanks and private corporations to challenge scientific evidence on a host of contemporary issues."[1] These issues begin with the scientific debates surrounding cigarette smoking, then move to nuclear deterrence methods, acid rain, the ozone hole, secondhand smoke, and lastly global warming. In each of these debates, we find new scientific discoveries producing concern among scientific communities and being met with resistance from scientists such as Singer and Seitz who used their "deep political connections" to "deliberately distort public debate" and run "effective campaigns to mislead the public and deny well established scientific knowledge for four decades."[2]

Part of what makes O&C's account effective is that they begin with the cigarette industry, which has been shown (via massive documentation) to care more about profits than health. This is about as villainous as it gets and, in retrospect, it is difficult to imagine how something now recognized as so immensely harmful could ever have been defended by scientists. O&C directly link these efforts to defend the cigarette industry to attacks on efforts to establish environmental regulations. It turns out that these attacks were often carried out by the very same scientists or organizations Seitz and Singer were involved with, marshaling increasingly aggressive methods and for similar reasons. Thus, although both Seitz and Singer are deceased, their methods, arguments, and rationale live on in contemporary climate denial.

Why did these men deny the dangers of cigarettes and oppose their regulation? It seems odd the scientists would vehemently oppose something that we now know to be good science. To understand why they did so, we need to understand something about their rationale.

12.2 WHY SUPPORT CIGARETTE COMPANIES AND OPPOSE ENVIRONMENTAL REGULATIONS?

Fred Seitz was active during the cold war and saw science and technology as the key to preserving American democracy and freedoms from communist Russia. He thought that environmentalists were "Luddites that wanted to reverse progress" and believed that Hollywood was morally corrupt.[3] Furthermore, the American masses didn't fully comprehend what they had and how much they owed to science and technology. Seitz also connected freedom to capitalism and was deeply concerned about attempts to regulate markets. Like Milton Freedman, he saw freedom as being connected to economic freedom, i.e., free markets. Thus regulating markets was a limitation of freedom and a move in the direction of communism.

Fred Singer seems to have agreed with this line of reasoning. He saw environmental efforts to establish regulations as an attack on the economy, which was an attack on freedom.[4] In short, America, democracy, freedom, capitalism, science, and technology belong together on one side, while regulation, big government, environmentalism, communism, corruption, and Hollywood belong on the other.

Interestingly, both men believed that scientists and academics were increasingly moving to the bad side: "Working scientists were finding more and more evidence that industrial emissions were causing widespread damage to human and ecosystem health. The free market was causing problems—unintended consequences—that the free market did not know how to solve. The government has a potential remedy—regulation—but that flew in the face of the capitalist ideal."[5] Since regulation was bad and free markets good, there *must* be a mistake somewhere. According to Seitz and Singer's logic, it was more likely that scientists were becoming corrupted than free markets were failing. Since their side couldn't be wrong, others must be wrong.

Ultimately, according to O&C, what we find here is a dogmatic market fundamentalism: the true faith must be defended. The ensuing "doubt-mongering campaigns" that Seitz, Singer, and others waged "were not about science. They were about the proper role of government, particularly in redressing market failures. Because the results of scientific investigation seem to suggest that government really did need to intervene in the marketplace if pollution and public health were to be effectively addressed, the defenders of the free market refused to accept those results. The enemies of government regulation of the marketplace became the enemies of science."[6]

Regulation is the boogeyman for market fundamentalists, which explains why Seitz would defend the tobacco industry: it had to be defended from regulation, from communism, from rejecting progress.

There is a fascinating need to deny certain realities in order to preserve this faith. O&C give the example of how, during the debates about establishing missile defense systems against Russia in the early 1980s, advocates of elaborate American defense systems insisted that Russia was advancing technologically and that the US must race ahead. Except when studies showed that Russians did not have certain technologies, these advocates insisted that evidence of the lack of these technologies was not a sign that they didn't have them, but that they must have technologies that cover up the technologies they must have! Bizarrely, the lack of evidence became evidence for what was not there.[7]

Similar arguments for the evidence that cigarette smoking was dangerous, both to smokers and later with regard to second-hand smoke, and that industrial pollution was causing acid rain and holes in the ozone, must be mistaken because this would imply that regulation was needed. Since regulation was evil, the scientists themselves must be making mistakes. They had lost their objectivity and become biased.[8]

This turn against science by these scientists did not stop with criticism, it turned into active campaigns against them. The methods developed in these campaigns have become even more widespread today.

12.3 THE METHODS OF DENIAL

What are these methods? When the scientific consensus didn't go their way, Seitz, Singer, and other market fundamentalist scientists cast doubt upon mainstream science. They accused it of losing objectivity, of being politically motivated, of being caught up in misguided social trends. In order to believe this, Seitz and Singer had to ignore evidence and deny the consensus that was coming from fields that were beyond their expertise. While many or most defenders of the cigarette industry might have done so cynically because they stood to profit, O&C think that market fundamentalists did so primarily for their ideological commitments more than for any profits they might gain. The cigarette industry was happy to have disgruntled scientists on their side and quickly used them to bolster their own case and attack the scientific consensus:

> For half a century the tobacco industry, the defenders of SDI [Reagan's Strategic Defense Initiative], and the skeptics about acid rain, the ozone hole, and global warming strove to 'maintain the controversy' and 'keep the debate alive' by fostering claims that were contrary to the mainstream of scientific evidence and expert judgment. They promoted claims that had already been refuted in the scientific literature, and the media became complicit as they reported these claims as if they were part of an ongoing debate.[9]

The primary goal was to manufacture doubt about the scientific consensus. This was done by casting doubt that there even was a consensus—although this claim was not effective against the scientific community. Seitz and Singer would try and get involved in scientific discussions, but they were not experts in these fields and those who were experts quickly saw that they were not motivated by truth, but by something else (their desire to defend free markets, which they took to be freedom). They were thus rejected by these scientific communities.

They then took their battle to the public. If they couldn't convince these scientists they were wrong, they could muddy the waters and seek to prevent both the government and the public from accepting the scientific consensus. Using their political connections and funded by wealthy interests, they sought to dress up their false claims as legitimate by presenting them in ways that looked and sounded scientific. Using "graphs, charts, references" and other things that looked and seemed scientific to the media and politicians, they claimed that the debate was not over, that there was reason to doubt the scientific consensus, that there was more evidence.[10] A common refrain was that more research was needed before any action could be taken. They also brought in experts from other fields, especially economics, who used various arguments to claim it was not economically feasible to fix these issues if they were true or that alternatives were not viable.[11] Politicians that shared their ideological commitments ate up these convenient claims and the media didn't seem capable of distinguishing the scientific consensus from the fake nonconsensus being pushed by the merchants of doubt.

It worked. Despite there being scientific consensus on many of these issues, even today a significant portion of the public still believes there is not. We continue to hear today that the science is incomplete and more research is needed, that the economic effects make change impractical, that mainstream science is biased, that these issues are so complicated we can't trust scientists, and that we should, in a word, doubt. O&C point out that part of the difficulty here is that science doesn't provide uncontestable truth. Even if the evidence is overwhelming, this does not mean that science is infallible. Science can make and has made mistakes. It is this space that the merchants of doubt seek to wiggle into and exploit. "There is no proof!" "We don't know for sure!" By fostering doubt and demanding we wait until we have proof, climate deniers are able to discourage action indeterminately. This perpetual pushing back of regulation and change tends to preserve the *status quo* and prevent the kind of radical change that is needed to genuinely deal with the environmental crisis.

12.4 FROM DOUBT TO OUTRIGHT LIES

The scientific consensus has only gotten stronger since O&C published *Merchants of Doubt*, but in some countries and in some political spheres the environmental crisis has become more politically polarized and the language has become even more fraught: in addition to claims that the consensus is not in or that the evidence is not clear, we hear that the "lamestream" media is biased and that anything that is inconvenient is "fake news"; global warming is a hoax, yet simultaneously air quality is better than it has ever been and no one cares more about the environment than some of the same people attacking it. Such political figures cut back environmental regulations and cut down social safety nets, all the while claiming to do more than anyone else previously to help any and all causes. Not only does there seem to be a complete disconnect from any reality beyond the reality that they assert, but supporters offer little resistance to outright lies and accept the most outlandish nonsense with little or no resistance.

It remains to be seen how this politicization will affect environmental issues in the future. The anti-environmental methods outlined by O&C did not go away with this political polarization; rather, they were augmented with outright lies. It is not clear if the lies will end when particular figures or political parties are replaced: there is a very real possibility that environmentalists will have to contend not with doubt-mongering but with ongoing blatant and manipulative lying.

12.5   A NOTE ON ARGUING ABOUT REALITY AND FACTS

One of the things to learn from this discussion is that as much as we would like to resolve arguments about environmental issues with data and facts, some interlocutors may be dogmatically committed to sowing doubt or caught up in "alternative facts." In such a debate, the conversation ends up with one side arguing that science has shown X, while the other side argues X has not been adequately proven.

A: "The data shows climate change is real."
B: "No, the data shows normal fluctuations in temperature."
A: "The scientific consensus is that we are dealing with a human-caused, abnormally fast increase in global temperature averages."
B: "Not all scientists agree: here, for example, is one who disagrees." Etc.

Depending on the degree of good faith of the interlocutors, an agreement might be reached if sufficient evidence or good argumentation are deemed convincing. But often these debates just go around and around and don't gain much traction. Such arguments often concern what is real or what are the facts, and they often rely on data and science. It should be noted that other registers are relevant to such a debate besides facts and reality.

One of these is the ethical register. Here the register of analysis is not What are the facts? or What is real? but rather What ought to be done? or What is moral? We can argue about whether or not manatees are endangered. But we could also argue that ethically we should protect animals even if they are not endangered. One question concerns the nature of reality, the other how we should act. Sometimes arguments about environmental issues get reduced to arguments about facts when they should also be about ethics. Thus, if A says, "There is still no adequate consensus on whether or not manatees are endangered," an appropriate response might be, "Even if there is not, it would still be morally correct to protect them in case it is true and likely even if it is not true." Too often the ethical register is sidelined while we wait for the facts to be resolved.

Yet another register is temporal. Some problems may not be an issue now but could be in the future. Nanobots might not exist—but they might be so dangerous that we should prevent or discourage the research that makes them possible. Genetic engineering might only exist in a rudimentary form, but it might have such potentially catastrophic consequences that we should not allow it. In each of these cases, a future possibility may require altering how we act now. Here again the issue is not the facts of the present, but the potential problems of the future.

The twentieth-century philosopher Hans Jonas argues that we have a moral responsibility toward the Earth and toward future generations of humans and nonhumans, but that we are often unaccustomed to including them in our political, social, and moral calculations. Especially because of the potentially catastrophic nature of some of our new or near technologies, he argues that we should privilege the "prophecy of doom" over the "prophecy of bliss."[12] Thus, while we can argue about the facts of climate change, the possibility of mass extinction is more than serious enough to warrant action, even if it turns out the situation is not as dire as the data seem to indicate.

12.6 AGAINST ENVIRONMENTALISM

There are clearly institutions and organizations that actively fight efforts to address and attempt to deal with various environmental crises. Some are crudely greedy and don't want to sacrifice profits. Others have less ignoble motivations. The scientists O&C discuss acted as they did because they associated markets with freedom and regulations with socialism. This is a political view, but also one that concerns human freedom and how society should be organized. In so doing, these scientists developed an approach that spreads doubt about scientific consensus and discourages much needed changes until these supposed doubts are resolved. Although this approach has proven very successful, it has been recently augmented with downright lies and deception.

To the degree that these efforts have been successful, they have spread a kind of learned ignorance that allows organizations and individuals to feel justified in not changing their ways, much less changing them radically. Some of this ignorance or indifference is inflicted, but some is tacit and inherent in our education and culture. The next chapters seek to examine the dynamics of epistemologies of ignorance and some of the major culture myths and narratives that prevent us from more adequately addressing climate change and mass extinction.

12.7 QUESTIONS FOR DISCUSSION

1. Why might scientists turn against scientific consensus?
2. Who spreads doubt about climate change and why? What are their methods for doing so?
3. Why are debates about environmental issues more complicated than just figuring out the facts?
4. What does it mean to privilege the "prophecy of doom" over the "prophecy of bliss"?

12.8 FURTHER READING

Obviously, the focus of this chapter is Oreskes and Conway's *Merchants of Doubt*, a seminal text worth further consultation. On the question of our responsibility to future generations of humans and nonhumans, see Jonas's *The Imperative of Responsibility*.

Notes

1 Oreskes, Naomi and Erik M. Conway. *Merchants of Doubt* (New York: Blooms-bury Press, 2011), 6.
2 Ibid., 241.
3 Ibid., 28.
4 Ibid., 134.
5 Ibid., 65.
6 Ibid., 262.
7 Ibid., 41.
8 Ibid., 61.
9 Ibid., 241.
10 Ibid., 244.
11 Ibid., 183.
12 Jonas, Hans. *The Imperative of Responsibility: In Search of an Ethics for the Technological Age* (Chicago, IL: University of Chicago Press, 1985).

13

EPISTEMOLOGY OF IGNORANCE AND THE ENVIRONMENTAL CRISIS

The previous chapter showed us that there are malicious, manipulative organizations and individuals that want to prevent us from taking the environmental crisis seriously. Their motivations for doing so vary from straightforward greed to political and ideological motivations such as preserving (market) freedoms. These organizations and individuals use various methods, including spreading doubt about science and scientific consensus, which muddies public discourse and aims to promote indifference and ignorance. Naturally, one of the ways for environmental advocates to seek to counter these efforts is by raising awareness. Sadly, these efforts are often met with a militant ignorance that is "aggressive, not to be intimidated, an ignorance that is active, dynamic, that refuses to go quietly—not at all confined to the illiterate and uneducated but propagated at the highest level of the land, indeed presenting itself unblushingly as knowledge."[1]

This kind of militant ignorance is not limited to organizations and individuals but can be widespread throughout many levels of society. While some do so for financial gain, there are good, intelligent people that do not take the environmental crisis seriously and may be entrenched in their indifference, but that at first glance don't seem to gain anything by doing so. What is happening here?

To understand this, let us look at Charles Mills's analysis of "epistemologies of ignorance," originally introduced in the context of race and institutional racism.

13.1 EPISTEMOLOGIES OF IGNORANCE

The very term "epistemology of ignorance" seems contradictory at first. "Epistemology" is the study of knowledge and of questions pertaining to knowledge. Often it centers on the kinds of methods we can use to obtain knowledge. Thus, an epistemology of ignorance seems to be the opposite of traditional epistemology: it seeks to understand ignorance or the lack of knowledge. As Mills makes clear, the problem, however, is not just ignorance, but ignorance that doesn't realize it is ignorance, ignorance that presents "itself unblushingly as knowledge."[2]

This problem is not new. Socrates famously accused the citizens of Athens of being more interested in money and fame than in truth and knowledge. In the allegory of the cave, Plato presents humankind as fettered inside a cave, trapped in their ignorance—as opposed to the few knowledgeable philosophers.

Unlike typical epistemology, Mills is concerned not with knowledge and how to gain it, but ignorance and how it functions, especially with regard to race. He is not the first to draw attention to ignorance—the German philosophical giant Kant portrays ignorance as the result of laziness and cowardice—but Mills's account shows the complexity of ignorance and how important the analysis of ignorance is for critical social issues.

The problem for Mills is "white ignorance." This concept is applicable to other countries, but Mills's focus is on the US. White ignorance entails a host of interrelated issues: 1. US history has been largely written by white (male) authors who have emphasized white (male) experience and perspectives; this leads to 2. the elision of nonwhite perspectives and experience from the collective memory, 3. entrenches white cultural and ethical norms, and 4. downplays the genocide and crimes inflicted on nonwhite people. Mills is not saying that all white people are ignorant in this regard, nor that all nonwhite people see through this. Nonwhite people can be caught up in white ignorance also. Mills is clear, however, that his approach is inspired by standpoint theory, which, as we saw in Chapter 7 with regard to ecofeminism, is the idea that those that are exploited or excluded by society are far more likely to be sensitive and knowledgeable about the injustices of that society. In a very real sense, they see it more clearly.

White ignorance is the inverse of the epistemic privilege of those who are exploited or excluded by society—it is being sheltered from having to think or recognize these issues. In the US, this manifests in the assertions that systematic racism does not exist, that racism is just a matter of a few bad eggs, that we need to teach "patriotic" (whitewashed) history in schools instead of "divisive" history that draws attention to historical crimes and racism, and, dramatically, that focusing on past and present racist injustice is itself racist. This bizarre inversion is perhaps best exemplified in the conviction held by some in the US that white people are the current victims of racism. Attempts to call out white ignorance and white complacency are cast as racist attacks on whites or attacks on America. Of course, these claims affirm exactly what they deny: that whiteness has been normalized.

Indeed, since 1997, when Mills wrote a book called *The Racial Contract*, the term "white privilege" has become popular again.[3] White privilege describes not only the social benefits of being white, but the ability of many white people to be ignorant of these advantages. Nonwhite individuals may seek the comfort of not thinking about these unpleasant issues, but as long as they have to survive in a predominantly white culture or in predominantly white communities, their blackness or brownness will prevent a full disappearance into whiteness (Barack Obama, for example, despite being raised by his white mother and grandparents, will always be perceived as black).

Importantly for Mills, white ignorance is learned. This is why he claims ignorance is not merely a lack of knowledge, but a kind of "structural group-based miscognition."[4] Recent Texas history textbooks refer to slaves as "workers." The genocide of Native Americans is often downplayed as an inevitable part of Manifest Destiny. The American Civil War is presented as not being fundamentally about slavery.[5] But white ignorance is not just taught in schools and in homes: it is "in the water," so to speak, and present in social norms and behavior. Having a name that doesn't sound "white" or speaking with an accent (obviously in addition to merely being nonwhite) can prevent one from getting a job, or selling a house, or can result in being treated differently by educators, the police, or hospitals. Alternatively, sounding or acting white can open doors that might otherwise be closed.

White ignorance intersects with many issues besides race. Take for example meritocracy, the belief that society is or ideally should be based on merit. This idea is attractive to many for multiple reasons, one of which is that when someone has succeeded financially, the claim that we live in a meritocracy affirms their productivity and moral uprightness. They have worked hard, and they have earned it. But if we assert that we do not have a meritocracy and that white privilege (and male privilege) play a role in success, this undermines the self-image of success being only or primarily due to hard work and uprightness. A white male who is not racist may find that his identity as an upright, hard worker has been attacked due to claims of systemic racism. All of a sudden he finds that his financial successes are being called into question and this might cut to the core of his being. Not surprisingly, he might lash out against claims of systemic racism not because he is racist, but because admitting such a reality seems to call into question the legitimacy of the very things he has relied on to feel like a moral person.

Ignorance, then, has its attractions. I can feel good about my country, good about who I am, and comfortable with the *status quo* precisely because my ignorance hides basic realities going on all around me. Mills's analysis is helpful for thinking about the ways that nonracists can ignore and reject acting on racism and therefore contribute to racism. This is an example of the kind of thing that results in what Eduardo Bonilla-Silva calls "racism without racists."[6] Bonilla-Silva is particularly concerned with claims of color-blindness. This is often lauded as a social and individual ideal: that we shouldn't see color. But as long as there are some people who are discriminating based on color and entrenched systematic racism, then seeking to not see color may do more damage than good. In the context of white ignorance, claims of color-blindness often function as excuses to not see and therefore not deal with racial disparities and racism.

13.2 TERRACIDE WITHOUT BIOPHOBIA

Epistemic ignorance is extremely relevant to the environmental crisis. It is significant that we have no equivalent to "racism" or "racists" in terms of environmental issues. Thus, the closest we can come to the idea of "racism without racists" is something like terracide without biophobia. "Killing the Earth without fearing and hating nature" is no less awkward than "anti-environmentalism without anti-environmentalists." The fact that we have no clear words to describe this phenomenon indicates the continuing low status of nature and the Earth in contemporary ethics and the fundamental anthropocentrism of modern society. In other words, the very lack of words shows how this phenomenon is so widespread.

While there may have been times in the past when particular groups or particular cultures demonstrated a hatred or antagonism toward nature (Gnosticism, for example), in modern industrialized countries, on the contrary, there is often an ostensive romanticization, appreciation, and commercialization of nature. The appreciation extends not only to cultivated nature (gardens, parks, zoos) but also wilderness and wild nature (wilderness preserves, museums, nature shows). Not everyone loves nature, but very few people hate it.

Despite this lack of biophobia, we are facing mass extinction and global climate change. The disparity between intent and outcome is even starker than in the case of racism. We know there are racists because some admit to being racists, while others let it slip in their language and behavior. There is someone to blame for racism, although focusing on overt racism elides tacit and systematic racism. But in the case of terracide, it is difficult to find someone to blame. Often corporations and politicians are blamed, and not entirely without reason, but even then, corporations and politicians are not acting out of biophobia, but rather out of greed or ideology or self-preservation.

Terracide without biophobia reveals something about our moral intuitions. As Zygmunt Bauman puts it,

> The scale of possible consequences of human actions have long outgrown the moral imagination of the actors. Knowingly or unknowingly, our actions affect territories and times much too distant for the 'natural' moral impulses which struggle in vain to assimilate them, or abandon the struggle altogether. Morality which we inherited from pre-modern times—the only morality we have—is a morality of proximity, and as such woefully inadequate in a society in which all important action is an action on distance.[7]

In the last chapter, we saw Hans Jonas's claim that ethics is not relevant merely to the present, but also to the future and to future generations of humans and nonhumans. Here Bauman elaborates Jonas argument that we are accustomed to thinking of morality as a matter of face-to-face human relations: don't lie, don't steal, don't kill. But, Bauman and Jonas argue, the reach of our technology is making it such that what I do here can affect someone on the other side of the Earth, nonhuman beings around the Earth, and both future humans and nonhumans. Moreover, the acts of many humans working in coordination or complexly disparately can have massive intended or unintended cumulative effects. One person buying a hamburger seems innocuous enough, but millions of people buying hamburgers can lead to massive rainforest deforestation worldwide. We are currently seeing floating islands of trash in the oceans, microplastics showing up in remote wilderness, mass extinction, and rising temperatures—and no one wants to take responsibility because no one is intending for this to happen. No single raindrop feels responsible for the flood.

Environmental advocates have long dealt with the difficulty of helping the public connect the dots and think ecologically. This is precisely what classic works like Carson's *Silent Spring* and Singer's *Animal Liberation* did: they showed the immorality of seemingly innocuous actions and the profound interconnections of humans to the world around them.[8]

While environmental philosophy has long identified anthropocentrism as a key contributor to ecological ignorance, the discussion of white ignorance makes it clear that any particular form of ignorance is often bolstered by a whole series of assumptions that may at first seem unconnected. A generally nonracist white man may refuse to recognize systematic racism because it undermines the supposed existence of a meritocracy on which he has built his sense of self-worth. Similarly, some men tie masculinity to destruction and resist any efforts labeled "green" because they find them "unmanly."[9] Or, as we saw in the last chapter, some scientists may refuse to accept scientific consensus because they find the implications for political policy intolerable. In one case, gender identity is driving environmental attitudes; in another, political ideology is doing so.

Ecological ignorance comes in different shapes and sizes and with complex moral valences. Combatting it requires an intersectional and philosophically sophisticated approach. It also requires close attention to the ways in which social and political issues are linked to what Charles Taylor calls the "sources of the self"—the complex tensions surrounding modern identity and modern moral narratives.[10] This is already difficult enough, but much public and political discourse tends to treat these issues as matters of scientific fact, and thus we end up with the absurd debates about the scientific consensus as described by Oreskes and Conway.

While it is beyond the scope of an introductory text to do justice to these complexities, it is important to discuss two of these nonenvironmental impediments to radical social change: economism and narratives of modern progress. These are both commonly invoked in response to efforts to alleviate the environmental crisis. The first argues that we can't do anything that will have serious negative economic effects and thus tends to shut down the possibility of radical change. The second tends to seek technological solutions and underemphasize the role of technology in creating the environmental crisis. They tend to preserve environmental ignorance.

13.3 QUESTIONS FOR DISCUSSION
1. What are "epistemologies of ignorance"?
2. How is epistemic ignorance a kind of inverse of epistemic privilege?
3. What is "racism without racists"? How is this concept applicable to environmentalism?
4. How can identity or political ideology contribute to environmental ignorance?

13.4 FURTHER READING
The classic work on epistemologies of ignorance is Charles Mills's *The Racial Contract*. An important collection of essays inspired by Mills is *Race and Epistemologies of Ignorance*. Eduardo Bonilla-Silva's *Racism without Racists* is another work that explores these issues.

Notes

1 Mills, Charles. "White Ignorance." In Sullivan and Tuana, eds., *Race and Epistemologies of Ignorance* (New York: State University of New York Press, 2007), 13.

2 Ibid.

3 The term was first popularized by Peggy McIntosh. See McIntosh, Peggy. "White Privilege: Unpacking the Invisible Knapsack." *Peace and Freedom Magazine* (July/August, 1989), 10–12.

4 Mills, Charles. "White Ignorance." In Sullivan, Shannon and Nancy Tuana, eds., *Race and Epistemologies of Ignorance* (New York: State University of New York Press, 2007), 13.

5 Turner, Cory. "Why Schools Fail to Teach Slavery's 'Hard History'." *NPR.*, 4 February, 2018.

6 Bonilla-Silva, Eduardo. *Racism without Racists: Color-Blind Racism and the Persistence of Racial Inequality in America*, 5th ed. (New York: Rowman & Littlefield, 2017).

7 Bauman, Zygmunt. *Postmodern Ethics* (Malden, MA: Blackwell, 1993), 217.

8 Carson, Rachel. *Silent Spring* (2002); Singer, Peter. *Animal Liberation* (2009).

9 Brough, Aaron R. and James E.B. Wilkie. "Men Resist Green Behavior as Unmanly." *Scientific American*, 26 December, 2017.

10 Taylor, Charles. *Sources of the Self: The Making of the Modern Identity* (Cambridge, MA: Harvard University Press, 1992).

14

MODERN MYTHS: ECONOMISM AND PROGRESS

Arguably the biggest impediment to dealing with the environmental crisis, along with anthropocentrism, is economism. For our purposes, economism is the privileging of the economic over the noneconomic. Currently, this tends to mean that a growing economy is more important than most other things, including the environment. Note that in defining economism in these terms I am taking a highly critical stance about economics and economic solutions to environmental problems. This is a radical position in the vein of deep ecology and radical environmentalism. Many environmentalists are open to economic incentivization and entrepreneurial approaches to environmental problems. Furthermore, big movements within economics, such as zero growth and degrowth, are currently pushing back against neoliberal economics. These movements are welcome and interesting, but it is not clear that they can overcome or mitigate the hegemony of capital. That is to say, while economic solutions may indeed be practical and are more likely to attract support, they are too often superficial or shallow.

Both anthropocentrism and economism are augmented by a strong faith in modern progress. The narrative of progress can not only inure us to the evils of the present ("better than it used to be"), but tends to seek technological solutions to what are often technological problems.

14.1 ECONOMISM

For the majority of human history, human societies centered on ritual, competition, play, art, storytelling, etc.[1] Only very recently has the economic become the primary concern. The ascent and triumph of the economic involved fighting directly against moral imperatives in multiple cultures that asserted the fundamental inhumanity and immorality of *auri sacra fames*—the lust for gold and money. But you wouldn't know this if you looked at the economic myths that have become ascendant.

Take for example the myth of economic progress. This is the claim that humankind has progressed through several periods of economic organization and that each shift is generally an improvement until the present, which is the best so far. This tends to denigrate the past and deify the present. On both counts it is wrong. First, regarding the past, the narrative of economic progress tends to paint the past as bad, and the further back one goes, the worse it gets. For example, hunter-gatherers are portrayed as wretched scavengers that are always on the brink of starvation, and agriculture is presented as a great leap forward from this misery. But the anthropological evidence shows not only that hunter-gathers were not miserable and starving, but that, on the contrary, they tended to be healthier than people living in agricultural civilizations.[2] Furthermore, they tend to be more egalitarian and happier than we are today.[3] The fact is that modern judgments of hunter-gatherers were biased and often racist.

If the narrative of economic progress led to such poor judgments of the past, what does this say for the praise of the present? Economists love to use economic measures such as GDP and measures of health such as life expectancy to claim that we are richer and healthier and therefore better off than ever before. Assuming this is true, these are definitely improvements. But life is much more than wealth and health. It is not clear that we live more meaningful lives—critics of capitalism and modernity have long claimed that many in modern society are alienated and exploited. Of course, this is an anthropocentric definition of life that overlooks the massive environmental damage done in modernity. This is not to say that humans have not done damage in the past; however, it is occurring on an unprecedented scale now.

Both economism and anthropocentrism focus attention away from the environment, and while economists and advocates of capitalism in general laud the benefits of capitalism for humankind, capitalism in particular, as Marx famously noted, is not about humans but capital. The capitalist drive for profit is insatiable. There is no natural stopping point in accumulating money and wealth: thousands? millions? Why stop? This is why the ancient world was so suspicious of money and merchants. Aristotle famously argued that seeking money can lead to a state of *pleonexia*—a kind of unhealthy addiction to accumulation. On these grounds, Plato recommended banning the merchants from the polis.[4] For Plato and Aristotle, human life should center on knowledge, truth, friendship, and character, not on the endless and potentially soul-damaging quest for money. In a very real sense, they worried that if the mercantile logic and temperament were to become widespread, it would mean an end to traditional forms of life that were not centered on money.

Indeed, as capitalism has been spread around the world, it always entails the radical alteration or destruction of traditional practices in favor of capitalist ones. In other words, humans have to be remade in the image of *homo economicus*—economic human.[5] Of course, to frame the shift in these terms challenges more myths of economism: the myth of barter and the myth that markets are natural.

The myth of barter is based on speculation by Adam Smith that the origin of money is rooted in the human propensity to barter with others. It became widespread in the late 1800s through the influence of Carl Menger.[6] The basic idea is that humans are naturally inclined to produce things and then exchange them. Originally they bartered, but this was time-consuming and they didn't always want what others had at the exact same time. Eventually, someone came up with the idea of a symbolic intermediary that could overcome these inefficiencies: money.

Whatever the intent of Smith's original account, it has become widely accepted in economics (and through it to larger audiences) as a statement on human nature: humans are economic animals. Not only this, however: on this account markets tend to emerge naturally. From this perspective, much of pre-capitalist history was marked by misguided limitations on markets. Only recently have we learned to free markets from the artificial shackles that fettered them, and we are now enjoying the benefits of free markets.

The problem with this history and these claims about human nature and markets is that they are flagrantly false. Anthropologists find no evidence of barter at all.[7] Furthermore, the anthropological and historical evidence is that markets do not emerge naturally and, on the contrary, often have to be forced on communities.[8] Despite the falsity of the myth of barter and the myth that markets are natural, both myths have proven highly resistant to challenges. This reflects not only the pseudo-scientific aura of economics, but also the deeply ideological nature of this vision of reality. Critics have compared this dogmatic economism to a cult.[9] Whether this is a fair characterization or not, economism certainly has friends in high places and tends to be politically accommodated on all sides.

This puts environmentalists in a difficult position because it tends to mean that environmental efforts need to be framed in economic terms or be economically friendly. Even in the 1970s, before the advent of extreme free market neoliberalism, Arne Naess claims that environmentalists were being forced to back off from their radical stances or be ostracized and ignored.[10] Environmentalism would have no place at the table unless it accepted playing second fiddle to economic concerns. Even today, when it is one or the other, economics wins.

This is not to say that the economy and the environment are complete and total opposites such that one cannot help the other without hurting it. Some entrepreneurs are seeking for ways to help the environment. Rather, the point is that if one has to budge for the other, it is almost always the environment that does the budging. The possibility of slowing the economy or even shrinking the economy, as the degrowth movement seeks, is heresy.

14.2 THE MYTH OF PROGRESS

Another contributing factor to the failure to address the environmental crisis is the myth of progress. We already have seen that the basic claim of the myth of progress is that the human condition is improving over time and that a shift from hunter-gatherers to agricultural societies is highly doubtful.

The claim of progress is broader than its application to economics. That claim is often tied to science and technology. Take for example the following passage:

> Francis Bacon, in the sixteenth century, was the first to foresee the physical power potential in scientific knowledge. We are the first, I am suggesting, to have enough of that power actually at hand to create new possibilities almost at will. By massive physical changes deliberately induced, we can literally pry new alternatives out of nature. The ancient tyranny of matter has been broken, and we know it. We found, in the seventeenth century, that the physical world was not at all like what Aristotle had thought and Aquinas had taught. We are today coming to the further realization that the physical world need not be as it is. We can change it and shape it to suit our purposes.
>
> Technology, in short, has come of age, not merely as technical capability, but as a social phenomenon. We have the power to create new possibilities, and the will to do so. By creating new possibilities, we give ourselves more choices. With more choices, we have more opportunities. With more opportunities, we can have more freedom, and with more freedom we can be more human. That, I think, is what is new about our age. We are recognizing that our technical prowess literally bursts with the promise of new freedom, enhanced human

dignity, and unfettered aspiration. Belatedly, we are also realizing the new opportunities that technological development offers to make new and potentially big mistakes.[11]

Here Emmanuel Mesthene presents a clear connection between science and technology. Science provides control over the physical world and this control enables the creation of technologies that are useful for humans. Not just useful but freeing. Freedom is explicitly tied to science and technology in this articulation.

But this should also cause us to hesitate. Freedom from what? Freedom from the "tyranny of matter." Freedom from the limitations of the physical world. Freedom won from and over nature, secrets wrestled from, as Merchant pointed out, *her*? Freedom, then—power to do to nature what we want, to shape it according to our desires, to our fantasies. On this account science, technology, and freedom seem united against nature, controlling it for our benefit.

This is rebellion. Nature is not seen as a bearer of gifts, as a loving mother, as the condition of our existence, but as an onerous limitation on our freedom and possibilities. Hannah Arendt noted that after the launch of the Soviet satellite Sputnik "the immediate reaction, expressed on the spur of the moment, was relief about the first 'step toward escape from men's imprisonment on Earth'."[12] There seems to be a kind of alienation from the Earth at work here: "Should the emancipation and secularization of the modern age, which began with a turning-away, not necessarily from God, but from a god who was the Father of men in heaven, end with an even more fateful repudiation of an Earth who was the Mother of all living creatures under the sky?"[13] We will explore the question of world and Earth alienation in Chapter 16.

It is also worth noting how Mesthene presents nature as fungible. He is not merely suggesting we use nature the way one uses seeds, sunlight, soil, and water to grow crops. The claim that we can "create new possibilities almost at will" suggests a radical fungibility—that nature can be so thoroughly undone as to disconnect what we can do with it from what it is. Nature is reduced to a nothingness from which we can proceed with our own creation ex nihilo. There is an ontological question here: What has nature become?

Lastly, after waxing ecstatic about these phenomenal cosmic powers, Mesthene, almost as an aside, mentions the potential for new and "big mistakes." This aside is, of course, telling. Technological optimism minimizes critical dangers. Importantly, because of this faith in science and technology, the solution to problems that may have been caused by technology tends to be new and improved technologies. This creates a loop where the only solution is technology. Criticism of technology or something like a technological paradigm gets dismissed as Luddism (hatred of technology).

Faith or optimism about science and technology doesn't tend to occur in the kind of stark framing and exuberance we see in the above passage from Mesthene. Rather, it is often just taken for granted. And it is precisely because it is taken for granted that it is difficult to discuss or implement changes that challenge the cycle of technological solutions.

Like in the previous discussion of economism, the claims about technological faith do not preclude important technological solutions; rather, one should point out that there is a tendency to slide into the STEM status quo and not question how STEM itself might be a part of the problem.

14.3 MODERN IDENTITY: FREEDOM, DIGNITY, AND POWER

Technology and economics can contribute to addressing the environmental crisis, but too often technological optimism and economism impede that process. Optimism about progress tends to obscure the depth of environmental problems and the role of technology in fomenting them, while also making us overconfident in technological solutions and complacent about making social changes (since some technology will surely save us). Economism has the startling power to disappear the non-economic, discourages us from making changes that would negatively affect the economy, and reduces possible responses beyond those limited to economic means (like creating incentives).

Anthropocentrism, economism, modern progress, STEM: these can become intertwined and reinforce each other. With regard to the environmental crisis, they too often function as an epistemology of ignorance that lulls us into a false sense of security. Speaking of the hold some of these ideas or paradigms seem to have on the modern imaginary *despite powerful criticisms against them*, the philosopher Charles Taylor asks a very important question: if these "arguments are so poor, what gives them their strength?" His response: "I believe that they derive their force from the *underlying image of the self,* and that this exercises its hold on us because of *the ideal of disengagement* and *the images of freedom, dignity and power* which attach to it...In short, its epistemological weaknesses are more than made up for by its moral appeal."[14] The moral appeal Taylor refers to is a tacit set of "ideals and interdicts of [modern] identity" that "shape our philosophical thought, our epistemology and our philosophy of language, largely without our awareness."[15]

We can see this at work in the above quotation from Mesthene, who directly ties science and technology to freedom, dignity, and power. In overcoming nature, humankind stands on its feet, proud, triumphant, and victorious. These ideas can be entwined with nationalism, gender, religion, aesthetics, etc. in complicated and sometimes contradictory ways. A healthy green lawn in the Arizona desert may be taken as a sign of manliness, patriotism, and religiosity. A monumental dam can be taken as a sign of progress, science, patriotism, power, and dignity.

There are spiritual and moral forces at work across these many permutations. For Taylor it is vital we do not pretend that even the most rigorously scientific studies can escape moral and spiritual meanings. While scientists may achieve objectivity in a lab, the moment these results are brought into the public sphere in human language, they are a part of a human world flush with moral valences and tensions. There is no way we can enumerate them all. There is no way to escape them.

For environmental philosophers and advocates, this means we must develop a sophisticated nuance regarding these moral and spiritual undertones and how they inform current debates, especially how ecological ignorance, anthropocentrism, economism, etc. will be leveraged to discourage the radical actions we now need.

14.4 QUESTIONS FOR DISCUSSION

1. What is economism?
2. What is the myth of barter? How does it give rise to the idea that markets are natural?
3. How does economism affect environmental efforts?
4. What is the myth of progress? How does it impede environmental efforts?
5. Why, despite the fact that anthropology has debunked these myths, do they retain such power over our imagination and self-understanding?

14.5 FURTHER READING

The best introduction to the anthropological critiques of these myths is David Graeber's impressive *Debt*. Another classic work is Marshall Sahlin's *Stone Age Economics*. Charles Taylor's *Sources of the Self* is an important work that points to the importance of narrative self-understanding for the modern reluctance to abandon some of these myths and explores the tensions in modern self-understanding.

Notes

1 Mumford, Lewis. "Tools Users vs. Homo Sapiens and the Megamachine." In Scharff, Robert C. and Cal Dusek, eds. *Philosophy of Technology* (Malden, MA: Wiley Blackwell, 2014), 381–88.

2 Scott, James C. *Against the Grain: A Deep History of the Earliest States* (New Haven, CT: Yale University Press, 2017).

3 Sahlins, Marshall. *Stone Age Economics* (Chicago, IL: Aldine-Atherton Inc., 1972).

4 Hénaff, Marcel. *The Price of Truth: Gift, Money and Philosophy* (Stanford, CA: Stanford University Press, 2010).

5 Castro Gomez, Santiago. "The Social Sciences, Epistemic Violence and the Problem of the 'Invention of the Other'." *Views from South*, vol. 3., no. 2 (2002), 269–85.

6 Smith, Adam. *An Inquiry into the Nature and Causes of the Wealth of Nations* (London: W. Strahan and T. Cadell, 1776). See also Menger, Carl. "On the Origins of Money." *The Economic Journal*, vol. 2, no. 6 (1892), 239–55.

7 Graeber, David. *Debt: The First 5,000 Years* (Brooklyn, NY: Melville House, 2014).

8 Ibid.

9 Cox, Harvey. *The Market as God* (Cambridge, MA: Harvard University Press, 2016); Boldeman, Lee. *The Cult of the Market: Economic Fundamentalism and Its Discontents* (Canberra, Australia: ANU E Press, 2011); McCarraher, Eugene. *The Enchantments of Mammon: How Capitalism Became the Religion of Modernity* (Cambridge, MA: Belknap Press, 2019).

10 Naess, Arne. "The Deep Ecological Movement: Some Philosophical Perspectives." *Philosophical Inquiry*, vol. 8, no. 102 (1986).

11 Mesthene, Emmanuel G. "The Social Impact of Technological Change." In Scharff, Robert C. and Cal Dusek, eds. *Philosophy of Technology* (Malden, MA: Wiley Blackwell, 2014), 681–82.

12 Arendt, Hannah. *The Human Condition* (Chicago, IL: University of Chicago Press, 1998), 1.

13 Ibid., 2.

14 Taylor, Charles. *Philosophical Papers: Volume 2, Philosophy and The Human Sciences* (New York: Cambridge University Press, 1985), 5–6. My italics.

15 Taylor, Charles. *Sources of the Self: The Making of the Modern Identity* (Cambridge, MA: Harvard University Press, 1992), ix.

15

THOUGHTLESSNESS AND THE ENVIRONMENTAL CRISIS

Why, if there is such a dire environmental crisis, is so little being done about it? The chapters in this section have covered contributing factors to this failure. This chapter will focus on thoughtlessness.

What is thoughtlessness and why is it relevant to the environmental crisis?

Broadly speaking, thoughtlessness is not thinking about what we are doing. This could be not thinking through the social, ethical, or moral implications of our actions. This could be a result of epistemic ignorance. It could refer to just going through the motions of our everyday routines mindlessly. Clearly, all these examples of thoughtlessness are major contributors to the environmental crisis.

But, as Hannah Arendt has shown, thoughtlessness can be much more sinister than this. Her account shows a particular form of thoughtlessness that arises in hyper-complex abstract systems—the kind of systems that are integral to modern society.

15.1 ARENDT ON THINKING AND THOUGHTLESSNESS

Arendt was a German-Jewish philosopher who had to flee Nazi Germany. One of the questions that preoccupied her after doing so was how Germany, despite being arguably the most scientifically and artistically advanced country in the world at the time, could democratically elect Adolf Hitler. With such brainpower in the country, why didn't more Germans try to stop him? Clearly, thinking was happening—but how could such a thoughtless result come from thinking?

The question of thinking and thoughtlessness pervades her writings, but her final, unfinished book, *The Life of the Mind*, offers a phenomenology of thinking. Simply put, she attempted to observe in very careful detail the phenomenon or act of thinking, especially with an eye to how it might differ from our typical understanding. She notes that there are different types of thinking despite our use of the word 'thinking' to encompass all of them.

One kind of thinking is problem-solving. We do this in countless circumstances: when a tool breaks, when lost in traffic, when doing schoolwork. Arendt points out that in many of these situations, we pull away from our immediate circumstances and withdraw into ourselves or the problem. When someone is working on a math problem, from the outside it may merely look like they are staring at it. We sometimes talk ourselves through a problem, muttering to ourselves, scribbling notes, or turning over a physical object in our hands. When we solve the problem, we stop thinking and return to the everyday world with the solution. Arendt calls this kind of thinking "cognition."

Another kind of thinking is wondering. We do this when we have found something surprising, new, awe-inspiring, or strange. Children often wonder about the world around them: why do birds eat bugs? Why is water blue? Why do people die? Like cognition, wonder also causes us to pause and stand back from what we were doing. Arendt claims that wondering is distinct from problem-solving because it is often concerned with questions of meaning. There may be a technical answer to the question "why do people die" that centers on the breakdown of the body, but the question is almost always one about what death means, not merely what physical mechanisms underlie it. Cognition attempts to solve a problem in relation to a certain set of circumstances, but wonder often questions the circumstances themselves. Thus, on Arendt's account, wondering often causes us to question the status quo while cognition tends to work within given constraints. Furthermore, wonder rarely offers solutions. There is rarely anything directly productive that comes from wondering. Perhaps confusingly, Arendt reserves for wonder the word 'thinking'.

There are also other forms of thinking on her account, such as contemplation (discussed in Chapter 2), but they need not concern us here. The key distinction for Arendt is between cognition and thinking (wonder). Distinguishing these two processes enables her to point to a particularly worrying kind of thoughtlessness: cognition without thinking (wonder) or, as I will call it, thoughtless cognition.

Why does this matter? Thoughtless cognition is extremely relevant for hyper-complex abstract systems. Take, for example, nuclear weapons. It requires impressive cognition to create them. But we might wonder whether we should create them at all. Are we ethically mature enough to handle them appropriately? For scientists with their nose in a complex fascinating problem, these questions may not intrude or may not intrude enough to stop the momentum of the project. Should genetic engineering be allowed? What can nanobots do? Often these issues are framed in terms of wisdom. We may be intelligent enough to do these things, but is it wise to do them?

However, the point is not just about wisdom for Arendt. The hyper-complex abstract systems of modern life are driven by profit, competition, and speed. As such, we actively discourage students and workers from wondering. It is useless. It is time-consuming and brings no tangible results. What we do need are problem solvers, students, and workers who can cognize. When we teach "critical thinking" we most often mean "efficient problem-solving skills." This emphasis on cognition is a fundamental change in the way we think in the accelerating machinery of modern life—and there are grave risks involved.

While wonder is often useless, it can have profound indirect effects. It can cause us to question the status quo. It can also cause us to question ourselves—and Arendt means this literally. Thinking as wonder can create an inner dialogue of me with myself.

[To myself]: "Why do you think that happened?"
[Responding to myself]: "I'm not sure. It was odd. What should we do?"
[Again to myself]: "Well, perhaps we should ..."

Arendt says that thinking in this way can initiate a divide with oneself and create a "2-in-1."[1] This other me is nothing short of a conscience. This is not to say that the other me is a saint, but that it creates a potentially healthy doubt and questioning. Now, from the perspective of a manager or perhaps even a teacher, the worker or student lost in thought is often a hassle. Parents know how annoying it can be to have a small child constantly distracted by bugs and wind and kites and cars while they are trying to get somewhere. So, we often hurry the child along and squash the wonder and the questions for some other time.

Let us look at a famous example to help us better understand thoughtless cognition.

15.2 EICHMANN

Arendt was present at the 1961 trial of Adolf Eichmann, who had been in charge of sending Jews to concentration camps. During the trial, Eichmann claimed that he did not hate Jews and argued that he was merely acting at the behest of his bosses. He had just done his job; it was his superiors who were responsible. The claim that he was just a cog in the machine did not go over well and the prosecution painted him as a monster. Arendt agreed that he was a monster, but she also accepted something of his claims to having just done his job. She noticed that he repeated clichés and at one point even attempted to invoke Kant's categorical imperative. He did shocking things, yes, but without the kind of malicious motives we might expect from someone doing such terrible things.

Eichmann's monstrosity was not in his malevolence but in the self-serving and ethically stunted excuses for his actions. Eichmann didn't want to kill Jews; he wanted a promotion. He didn't relish doing what he was told, but if he didn't do it, someone else would. Despite his participation in great evil, Eichmann was disappointingly ordinary. Arendt called this the "banality of evil." Evil can be done by murderous villains, but it can also be done by cowardly bureaucrats that keep the machinery running instead of resisting it. Eichmann was good at solving the logistical problems involved in efficiently sending Jews to their death. In other words, he was highly competent in terms of cognition. But he was deeply thoughtless. Eichmann, then, for Arendt, is paradigmatic of thoughtless cognition.

Her book *Eichmann in Jerusalem* was highly controversial,[2] in part because she didn't limit her analysis to Eichmann but pointed to the ways that this thoughtless cognition and banality of evil were widespread in modern society. Arendt believed that, in the same way that prosecutors assumed Eichmann must be a malevolent monster, many Germans had put the blame on Hitler and the Nazis for the Holocaust and completely failed to take responsibility for their own complicity. They may not have killed Jews with their own hands, but they said nothing when Jews were taken away. Now, after the war, they were allowing Nazi soldiers to return to normal life and seemingly excused them for the same reason Eichmann sought to excuse himself. Thus Arendt uncomfortably implied that there were many like Eichmann around the world: competent but thoughtless people who can make the trains run on time, but who are ethically stunted and fundamentally irresponsible.

15.3 MILGRAM'S SHOCK BOX

Arendt's analysis of the banality of evil challenges the comforting assumption that the world is made of bad guys and good guys. Alarmed by her claims, the psychologist Stanley Milgram designed a now-infamous experiment aimed specifically at exploring obedience and authority. Subjects were asked to pose questions to a "learner" in another room, who (unbeknownst to the subjects) was an actor following the instructions of Milgram and his colleagues. If the learner's answer was wrong, the subject was instructed to administer initially weak but progressively stronger electric shocks. Their shock box was clearly marked so that they could see when the shocks they supposedly administered reached a dangerous level of intensity. Meanwhile, the learner, who wasn't actually being shocked, would make the appropriate sounds of pain and torment in response to the subject's actions. An "experimenter" would stand nearby and respond to concerns from subjects with reassuring comments aimed at keeping the experiment going.

In the initial study, 25 of the 40 subjects went all the way to the highest level of shock.[3] In similar versions of the experiment, up to 85% of subjects went that far. Milgram's conclusions are disconcerting: "Ordinary people, simply doing their jobs, and without any particular hostility on their part, can become agents in a terrible destructive process. Moreover, even when the destructive effects of their work become patently clear, and they are asked to carry out actions incompatible with fundamental standards of morality, relatively few people have the resources needed to resist authority."[4]

Milgram also affirms the ways in which the hyper-complex abstract systems of modernity contribute to this thoughtlessness and moral stunting:

> The problem of obedience is not wholly psychological. The form and shape of society and the way it is developing have much to do with it. There was a time, perhaps, when people were able to give a fully human response to any situation because they were fully absorbed in it as human beings. But as soon as there was a division of labor things changed. Beyond a certain point, the breaking up of society into people carrying out narrow and very special jobs takes away from the human quality of work and life. A person does not get to see the whole situation but only a small part of it, and is thus unable to act without some kind of overall direction. He yields to authority but in doing so is alienated from his own actions.
>
> Even Eichmann was sickened when he toured the concentration camps, but he had only to sit at a desk and shuffle papers. At the same time the man in the camp who actually dropped Cyclon-b into the gas chambers was able to justify his behavior on the ground that he was only following orders from above. Thus there is a fragmentation of the total human act; no one is confronted with the consequences of his decision to carry out the evil act. The person who assumes responsibility has evaporated. Perhaps this is the most common characteristic of socially organized evil in modern society.[5]

15.4 IMPLICATIONS FOR THE ENVIRONMENTAL CRISIS

What does this mean for the environmental crisis?

Broadly speaking, thoughtlessness has always been a central concern of environmentalists. Rachel Carson's *Silent Spring* sought to wake people up to the environmental problems caused by pesticides. Peter Singer's *Animal Liberation* sought to raise awareness of the unethical treatment of animals used for consumption. The very structure of many similar environmental books and articles is based on the assumption that people are not fully aware of what is happening and that they need consciousness-raising. The aim is to move the public or as many individuals as possible from thoughtlessness to thoughtfulness.

Environmentalists have long been aware of the banality of evil with regard to environmental issues. Many environmental issues are caused not by maliciousness, but by the accumulation of careless or thoughtless acts. Littering is often done out of laziness and indifference. Destruction of wet-lands is done out of a desire for "productive" land rather than from hatred of waterfowl. As we saw in Chapter 13, this phenomenon could be called "terracide without biophobia." Much environmental damage is due to a desire to help human flourishing. Anthropocentrism elides or disappears the direct and indirect consequences of human action. Hence many environmental actions are designed to make animal suffering and environmental destruction visible.

Arendt's analysis of thoughtless cognition alerts us to the structural and systematic aspects of contemporary thoughtlessness. We live in a cultural atmosphere with deeply ingrained commitments to productivity and problem-solving. We are discouraged from thinking (wonder) and everywhere encouraged to productively cognize solutions to problems. Efficient cognition is widely mistaken for critical thinking. As a result, we think we are thinking, when we may actually be producing a dangerous thoughtless cognition. We think that thinking means producing more and solving more problems (cognition), when this may actually be a form of thoughtlessness. We may be mistaking part of the problem for the solution. Our (cognitive) thinking remains caught within the status quo.

To be clear, Arendt does not claim that thinking (wonder) inevitably eliminates thoughtlessness or inevitably promotes the development of a conscience. She suggests it can contribute to doing this, but stresses that this is by no means the entire issue. If there is an opposite of thoughtlessness, it is perhaps good or wise judgment. The third volume of Arendt's *The Life of the Mind* was meant to examine judgment, but she died before writing it.[6] As a result, we can only speculate about how judgment is a positive contrast to thoughtlessness. We are left merely with a diagnosis of the problem of thoughtlessness.

If Arendt is correct about thoughtless cognition, then the task of consciousness-raising is far more difficult. It is already difficult enough to unravel the tacit moral and spiritual strands that link anthropocentrism, economism, and progress to identity and strengthen modern ecological ignorance, but many of our workplaces, educational spaces, and institutions discourage thinking (wonder) while simultaneously assuring us that we are critical thinkers (cognition).

15.5 QUESTIONS FOR DISCUSSION

1. What are the different kinds of thinking according to Arendt?
2. What is thoughtless cognition? Why is it dangerous?
3. What are the implications of this analysis for environmental philosophy? How does thoughtless cognition complicate the environmental crisis?

15.6 FURTHER READING

Both Arendt's *The Life of the Mind* and *The Human Condition* deal with the issue of thoughtlessness (as many of her works do). The argument presented in this chapter is made in greater detail in my *How the Neoliberalization in Academia Leads to Thoughtlessness.*

Notes

1 Arendt, Hannah. *The Life of the Mind* (New York: Harcourt Brace Jovanovich, 1978).
2 Arendt, Hannah. *Eichmann in Jerusalem* (New York: Penguin Classics, 2006).
3 Milgram, Stanley. "The Perils of Obedience." *Harper's*, vol. 247, no. 1483 (December 1973), 62–77.
4 Ibid., 75–76.
5 Ibid., 77.
6 Arendt, Hannah. *Lectures on Kant's Political Philosophy* (Chicago, IL: University of Chicago Press, 1992).

16

WORLD ALIENATION AND *AMOR MUNDI*

We live in desperate times. Scientists have been blaring alarms for years and yet nothing seems to change. Temperatures are rising, plant and animal species are dying off, yet some deny there is climate change at all. For many, these issues don't matter unless they affect humans. Some do seek change, but do not want to slow economic growth. Others seek technological solutions. Epistemological ignorance and thoughtlessness lock us into complacency.

Altogether, this reflects a fundamental world alienation. As a concluding provocation, I want to suggest we need *amor mundi*—love of the world. This topic brings this book full circle, as world alienation and *amor mundi* were fundamental concerns introduced in the first two chapters.

16.1 WORLD ALIENATION

Alienation is normally associated with Karl Marx, for whom it describes the condition of workers in factories.[1] These individuals work for long hours doing repetitive tasks. They have no influence over the kind of product manufactured, how it is made, or what is done with it. They are simply paid to do what they are told. For Marx, this is alienating in two ways. First, they are alienated from the product they are making and second, they are alienated from themselves. Alienation here means "made strange" or "estranged." Workers have no control over the product they are making. They have no control over themselves. They have sold their body to make something for someone else. They are thus divorced from both the fruits of their labor and their labor, but also estranged from themselves (their desires, their bodies) and reduced to objects making objects.

World alienation, then, means to be divorced from the world, or that the world has become estranged or made strange to us. In *The Human Condition*, Hannah Arendt distinguishes between world alienation and earth alienation.[2] By world, she means a human world, the way we might describe the Roman world or the world of ancient Egypt. Such a human world refers to the traditions, customs, history, language, architecture, morals, aesthetics, etc., that one is born into. Arendt believes our modern individualism and our consumerism are eating up and destroying human worlds. She also briefly discusses Earth alienation, which she saw evinced in language around the rise of space exploration—specifically in the calls to escape the Earth, which she oddly cast as a prison.

Native Americans are one of the groups that have been consistently critical of the Western tradition in this regard. But for Native Americans like Deloria, Wildcat, and Wall Kimmerer, world alienation is especially alienation from the natural world, from the plants, animals, and other beings of a particular place. Deloria claims that this alienation from the natural world is now affecting young Native Americans:

> In the modern period, Indians [sic] are in tremendous transition because we are going through your educational system, wherein we move away from the specifics of the universe traditional Indians lived with and we move toward the scientific way of thinking. Many Indian people are leaving their culture and traditions in ways they do not suspect. They are developing a schizophrenia. They look at their grandfather, who goes out and talks with birds and coyotes, and they think he is superstitious. And yet they go to school and they learn that they are supposed to love nature and learn from nature. So we are getting, in my opinion, a generation of lost Indians who are going out there, just like lost whites, and trying to embrace trees and think this is doing something Indian.[3]

As we saw in the first chapter, Deloria and Wildcat claim that Western ontology (the Western way of understanding the nature of reality) treats the physical world as a complex system of mere objects, as if it were mechanical or dead. But Native American ontology sees not only plants and animals as alive, but also the wind, water, rocks, and entire landscapes. On Deloria's account, young Native Americans are being taught science and Western ontology in schools and forget that the world is alive. When they see their grandfather talking to the "birds and coyotes" they are alienated from this experience, which seems strange to them. They have become divorced from the living cosmos.

Perhaps the most obvious sign of this alienation from the natural world, as Wall Kimmerer points out, is to not know the names of things, much less their personalities.[4] Not surprisingly this alienation produces deeply unethical relationships with the natural world. As Osage chief Big Soldier put it in 1820,

> I see and admire your manner of living, your good warm houses, your extensive fields of corn, your gardens, your cows, oxen, workhouses, wagons, and a thousand machines that I know not the use of. I see that you are able to clothe yourselves, even from weeds and grass. In short, you even do almost what you choose. You are surrounded by slaves. Everything about you is in chains, and you are slaves yourselves. I fear if I should exchange my pursuits for yours, I too should become a slave.[5]

Deloria believes some "lost whites" have realized this, and they often come to Native Americans looking to find nature and themselves. He claims this desire for wholeness is still caught up in the estrangement of alienation:

> For the most part Indians do not 'deal with' or 'love' nature. In the Western European context human experience is separated from the environment. When Indians are told that they 'love nature,' they cannot deal with this because nature is not an abstraction to them.
>
> Indians do not talk about nature as some kind of concept or something 'out there.' They talk about the immediate environment in which they live. They do not embrace all trees or love all rivers and mountains. What is important is the relationship you have with a particular tree or a particular mountain.[6]

In this fascinating passage Deloria rejects the idea that Native Americans love "nature" or the "Earth." These are abstractions. Native Americans have a "relationship" with a "particular tree" or a "particular mountain." From his perspective the desire to love and reunite with "nature" is itself a reflection of a state of alienation. Problematically, the attempt at reconciliation is too often abstract and thus doesn't deal with the particular beings around us. The entire conceptual framework that casts nature as an abstract thing from which one is separated and needs to reconcile with and love strikes Deloria as reflecting this deep alienation.

This separation from the world is not just spiritual, ontological, or mental. Wildcat points out that it is a physical alienation:

> Automobiles, television, air conditioning, and computers, to pick four obvious examples, result in human convenience, entertainment, comfort, and escape from incredible drudgery. But I interact less directly and physically in time and space with other human beings and the natural environment because of the ease, comfort, privacy or relative isolation with which I can use these technologies. Technology, in general, has reshaped most people's everyday lives, often in measurably positive ways. But here is the irony: as we disengage technology from communities (which include plants, animals, and geographic/geologic features) with a sense of place, and thereby create cultures and forms of communication that are relatively abstract, we unconsciously destroy conditions for our human survival and threaten the lives of many other plants and animals with whom we share this biosphere.[7]

Science and technology have allowed many individuals to physically separate themselves from the limits of natural time and space. We produce foods out of season that can be shipped far from where they would naturally grow. In fact, in many ways the modern grocery store is the embodiment of modern world alienation. We can buy all kinds of foods but don't know where they came from, when they were produced, who grew and picked them. This is abstract food in an abstract economy.

Given the predominance of economic and anthropocentric concerns in modern society, world alienation is simply not a concern for most people. This means it is less obtrusive than the kind of alienation Marx describes, although even the alienation of labor has been made less uncomfortable and unpalatable over the last 100 years. While world alienation may damage our souls and threaten the world itself, we can perform our labor in air-conditioned comfort.

16.2 OVERCOMING WORLD ALIENATION: *AMOR MUNDI*

What would be the opposite of world alienation? I want to propose, as a provocation, an opposite to world alienation: *amor mundi*. This term comes from Hannah Arendt, who in turn offers it as a foil to an earlier German philosopher, Friedrich Nietzsche, and his concept of *amor fati*.[8] Briefly, Nietzsche believed that the project of modernity had failed and that it has resulted in a state of nihilism, a widespread cultural decline that culminates in a vacuous consumer society. To overcome this nihilism, he offered a challenge and a solution: *amor fati,* the love of (one's) fate. Nietzsche believed that instead of seeking to eliminate all aspects of life we don't like (an impossible task), we must learn to love all aspects of life, both the ugly and the beautiful. For Nietzsche, a healthy person and a healthy society must embrace all of life and affirm it, whereas an unhealthy person and an unhealthy society are beaten down and exhausted by life.

Arendt viewed Nietzsche's account as too individualistic (a criticism she also leveled at a movement called existentialism), but she liked the emphasis on love. Arendt believed that what we need to love is not primarily our fate, but our world. As we saw earlier, Arendt distinguishes between "Earth" and "world," the latter referring to human worlds, such as "the world of ancient Egypt." Thus, Arendt's concept of *amor mundi* is anthropocentric. But if we use "world" to refer not to the human world but to the Earth, the environment, and/or specific places and their nonhuman peoples, then this *amor mundi* is a powerful foil to world alienation.

While world alienation doesn't know the name of things, doesn't know the history or personality of places, doesn't know where food comes from and may see the natural world as an object to be exploited, *amor mundi* seeks to do the opposite. It learns the history, names, and personality of place, cares about food, and fights exploitation. It sees that we are all interconnected and that what we do affects peoples and things on the other side of this Earth. When there is a metaphysics that sees nature as our Mother (Chapter 3) or nonhuman beings as our older siblings (Chapter 1), this *amor mundi* may be more deeply felt.

Let me speak to this point on a personal level. I read Vine Deloria Jr. while in graduate school and was impressed with the implications of Indigenous ontology as he described it. I am not Native American, and I recognize that Native American traditions are far more complicated than just the metaphysics Deloria outlines. But Deloria's description of power and place deeply affected me. I found myself seeking to learn more about the names, history, and rhythms of the world around me. My experience of the natural world was enhanced, as was my understanding of ethics. I am not claiming that we can put on or take off our metaphysical understanding of the world as if it were clothing. World alienation doesn't go away once one is exposed to the living cosmos. My point is that there is power in the idea of a living cosmos. In saying this I am not repeating Deloria's claim about the reality of power in the living cosmos; I am saying that even the idea itself can be unsettling or dislodging in important ways.

I should also note that, as we saw earlier, Deloria explicitly resists the idea that Native Americans love nature or the Earth. There are two problems here. He finds the idea of "nature" or "Earth" to be abstract and claims that

Native Americans interact with specific beings in specific places. The issue here is that Western abstract (and often world-alienated) concepts are being imposed on Indigenous traditions and practices. The same is true of the word "love." Love in the West has a certain history, including a connection with emotions. The Romantic Western stereotype of the Native American's idyllic relationship with nature is deeply flawed. If it is appropriate to speak of a "love" of "nature", "love" needs to be heard more closely to "respect" specific nonhuman beings. A personal relationship with a river or a bear can involve both care and also an appropriate fear and respect.

I could say much more about what *amor mundi* would look like and have attempted to explore these nuances elsewhere.[9] I invoke it here at the end of this book as a provocation. *Amor mundi* is not meant to be the definitive alternative to world alienation, but rather a tool to help us banish our complacency. If we understand *amor mundi* broadly, I believe it can be a valuable lens that allows us to see the ways in which we are alienated from the world. Thus, this is the question I hope to leave readers to ponder: *If we loved the world and the nonhuman peoples in it, how would we act differently?*

16.3 DESPERATE TIMES

The first section of this book questioned whether there was something about the project of modernity that made it uniquely dangerous to the environment. Humans have, after all, caused environmental damage before—but never on this scale. Over the course of the preceding chapters, we have looked at many of the criticisms and suggestions regarding what needs to change.

We live in desperate times. Climate denial, ignorance, economism, thoughtlessness, and world alienation prevent us from internalizing the depth of that desperation. There is no single solution, no deus ex machina that can save us. We don't even realize the critical nature of the problem. I hope that asking Why not? will help us do so.

16.4 QUESTIONS FOR DISCUSSION

1. What is world alienation?
2. Why does Deloria resist saying Native Americans love nature or the Earth?
3. Arendt believes we are too individualistic and that *amor mundi* might help us overcome that individualism. Explain.
4. If Arendt's call for *amor mundi* is applied to environmental concerns, might it help develop ecological thinking?
5. *If we loved the world and the nonhuman peoples in it, how would we act differently?*

16.5 FURTHER READING

See Chapter 1 for additional readings from a Native American perspective. The argument about the importance of *amor mundi* introduced here is presented in further detail in my *Amor Mundi and Overcoming Modern World Alienation*.

Notes

1 Tucker, Robert C., ed. *The Marx–Engels Reader* (New York: W.W. Norton, 1978).

2 Arendt, Hannah. *The Human Condition* (Chicago, IL: University of Chicago Press, 1998).

3 Deloria, Jr., Vine. "Kinship with the World." *Journal of Current Social Issues*, vol. 15, no. 3 (Fall 1978), 19–21.

4 Wall Kimmerer, Robin. *Braiding Sweetgrass: Indigenous Wisdom, Scientific Knowledge and the Teaching of Plants* (Minneapolis, MN: Milkweed Editions, 2015).

5 Deloria, Jr., Vine. *Spirit and Reason: The Vine Deloria, Jr., Reader* (Golden, CO: Fulcrum, 1999), 4.

6 Deloria, Jr., Vine. "Kinship with the World." *Journal of Current Social Issues*, vol. 15, no. 3 (Fall 1978), 19–21.

7 Deloria, Jr., Vine and Daniel Wildcat. *Power and Place: Indian Education in America* (Golden, CO: Fulcrum, 2001), 76.

8 Nietzsche, Friedrich. *The Gay Science* (New York: Vintage, 1974).

9 Pack, Justin. *Amor Mundi and Overcoming Modern World Alienation* (Lanham, MD: Lexington Books, 2020).

REFERENCES

Adams, Carol J. *The Sexual Politics of Meat: A Feminist-Vegetarian Critical Theory*. New York: Bloomsbury, 2015.

Arendt, Hannah. *Eichmann in Jerusalem*. New York: Penguin Classics, 2006.

——. *The Human Condition*. Chicago: University of Chicago Press, 1998.

——. *Lectures on Kant's Political Philosophy*. Chicago: University of Chicago Press, 1992.

——. *The Life of the Mind*. New York: Harcourt Brace Jovanovich, 1978.

Bauman, Zygmunt. *Postmodern Ethics*. Malden, MA: Blackwell, 1993.

Berry, Wendell. *Bring It to the Table: On Farming and Food*. Berkeley, CA: Counterpoint, 2009.

Birch, Thomas H. "The Incarceration of Wilderness: Wilderness Areas as Prisons." In *The Great New Wilderness Debate*, ed. J. Baird Callicot and Michael P. Nelson. Athens, GA: University of Georgia Press, 1998.

Boldeman, Lee. *The Cult of the Market: Economic Fundamentalism and Its Discontents*. Canberra, Australia, ANUE Press, 2011.

Bonilla-Silva, Eduardo. *Racism without Racists: Color-Blind Racism and the Persistence of Racial Inequality in America*. 5th ed. New York: Rowman & Littlefield, 2017.

Brague, Rémi. *The Wisdom of the World: The Experience of the Universe in Western Thought*. Chicago: University of Chicago Press, 2003.

Brough, Aaron R. and James E.B. Wilkie. "Men Resist Green Behavior as Unmanly." *Scientific American* (26 December 2017).

Callicot, J. Baird, and Michael P. Nelson, eds. *The Great New Wilderness Debate*. Athens, GA: University of Georgia Press, 1998.

Carrington, Damian. "Humanity has wiped out 60% of animal populations since 1970, report finds." *The Guardian*, 30 October, 2018.

————. "Plummeting insect numbers 'threaten collapse of nature'." *The Guardian*, 10 February, 2019.

Carson, Rachel. *Silent Spring*. Boston, MA: Houghton Mifflin Company, 2002.

Castro Gomez, Santiago. "The Social Sciences, Epistemic Violence and the Problem of the 'Invention of the Other'." *Views from South*, vol. 3, no. 2 (2002): 269–85.

Cox, Harvey. *The Market as God*. Cambridge, MA: Harvard University Press, 2016.

Curtin, Deane. "Women's Knowledge as Expert Knowledge: Indian Women and Ecodevelopment." In *Ecological Feminism: Multidisciplinary Perspectives*, ed. Karen Williams. Bloomington, IN: Indiana University Press, 1997, 82–98.

Deloria, Vine, Jr. "Kinship with the World." *Journal of Current Social Issues*, vol. 15, no. 3 (Fall 1978): 19–21.

————. *Spirit and Reason: The Vine Deloria, Jr., Reader*. Golden, CO: Fulcrum, 1999.

————. *We Talk, You Listen: New Tribes, New Turf*. Lincoln, NE: Bison Books, 1997.

Deloria, Vine, Jr., and Daniel Wildcat. *Power and Place: Indian Education in America*. Golden, CO: Fulcrum, 2001.

Devall, Bill. "The Deep Ecology Movement." *National Resources Journal*, vol. 20, no. 2 (1980): 219–303.

Devall, Bill, and George Sessions. *Deep Ecology: Living as if Nature Mattered*. Kaysville, UT: Gibbs Smith, 2007.

Dodge, Jim. "Living by Life: Some Bioregional Theory and Practice." In *Home! A Bioregional Reader*, ed. Van Andruss, Judith Plant, et al., Gabriola, BC: New Society Publishers, 1990: 5–12.

Estabrook, Barry. "Politics of the Plate: The Price of Tomatoes." *Gourmet* (March 2009).

Estévez-Saá, Margarita, and María Jesús Lorenzo-Modia. *The Ethics and Aesthetics of Eco-caring: Contemporary Debates on Ecofeminism(s)*. New York: Routledge, 2020.

Federici, Silvia. *Re-Enchanting the World: Feminism and the Politics of the Commons*. Oakland, CA: PM Press, 2018.

Food Chains. Directed by Sanjay Rawal, Screen Media, 2014.

Fox, Michael Allen. "Vegetarianism and Treading Lightly on the Earth." In *Environmental Ethics: Readings in Theory and Application*, ed. Louis P. Pojman et al., Boston, MA: Wadsworth Publishing, 2016, 533–41.

Gaard, Greta, and Lori Gruen. "Ecofeminism: Toward Global Justice and Planetary Health." *Society and Nature*, vol. 2 (1993): 1–35.

Gilligan, Carol. *In a Different Voice: Psychological Theory and Women's Development*. Cambridge, MA: Harvard University Press, 2009.

Graeber, David. *Debt: The First 5,000 Years*. Brooklyn, NY: Melville House, 2014.

Griswold, Eliza. "How 'Silent Spring' Ignited the Environmental Movement." *New York Times Magazine*, 21 September, 2012.

Guha, Ramachandra. "Radical American Environmentalism and Wilderness Preservation: A Third World Critique." In *The Great New Wilderness Debate*, ed. J. Baird Callicot and Michael P. Nelson, Athens, GA: University of Georgia Press, 1998.

Hénaff, Marcel. *The Price of Truth: Gift, Money and Philosophy*. Stanford, CA: Stanford University Press, 2010.

Hobbes, Thomas. *Hobbes: On the Citizen*. New York: Cambridge University Press, 1998.

Honoré, Carl. *In Praise of Slowness: Challenging the Cult of Speed*. New York: Harper One, 2005.

IPCC, "Summary for Policymakers." In *Global warming of 1.5°C. An IPCC Special Report on the impacts of global warming of 1.5°C above pre-industrial levels and related global greenhouse gas emission pathways, in the context of strengthening the global response to the threat of climate change, sustainable development, and efforts to eradicate poverty*, ed. Masson-Delmotte, Zhai, et al. In press.

Johnson, Kevin. "The Southwest Is Facing an 'Unprecedented' Migratory Bird Die-Off." *Audubon*, 16 September, 2020.

Jonas, Hans. *The Imperative of Responsibility: In Search of an Ethics for the Technological Age*. Chicago, IL: University of Chicago Press, 1985.

———. *The Phenomenon of Life: Toward a Philosophical Biology*. Evanston, IL: Northwestern University Press, 2001.

Kittay, Eva Feder. *Love's Labor: Essays on Women, Equality and Dependency*. New York: Routledge, 1999.

Kolbert, Elizabeth. *The Sixth Extinction: An Unnatural History*. New York: Henry Holt and Co., 2014.

Kuhn, Thomas. *The Structure of Scientific Revolutions*. Chicago: University of Chicago Press, 1996.

Leopold, Aldo. *A Sand County Almanac: And Sketches Here and There*. New York: Oxford University Press, 2020.

Little, Margaret Olivia. "Why a Feminist Approach to Bioethics?" *Kennedy Institute of Ethics Journal*, vol. 6, no. 1 (1996): 1–18.

Matthews, Freya. "Becoming Native: An Ethos of Countermodernity II." *Worldviews: Environment, Culture, Religion*, vol. 3, no. 3 (1999): 243–72.

McCarraher, Eugene. *The Enchantments of Mammon: How Capitalism Became the Religion of Modernity*. Cambridge, MA: Belknap Press, 2019.

McIntosh, Peggy. "White Privilege: Unpacking the Invisible Knapsack." *Peace and Freedom Magazine* (July/August 1989): 10–12.

Menger, Carl. "On the Origins of Money." *The Economic Journal*, vol. 2, no. 6 (1892): 239–55.

Merchant, Carolyn. *The Death of Nature: Women, Ecology and the Scientific Revolution*. New York: Harper and Row, 1990.

Mesthene, Emmanuel G. "The Social Impact of Technological Change." In *Philosophy of Technology*, ed. Robert C. Scharff and Cal Dusek, Malden, MA: Wiley Blackwell, 2014, 681–82.

Milgram, Stanley. "The Perils of Obedience." *Harper's*, vol. 247, no. 1483 (December 1973): 62.

Mills, Charles. "White Ignorance." In *Race and Epistemologies of Ignorance*, ed. Shannon Sullivan and Nancy Tuana, New York: State University of New York Press, 2007, 13–38.

Muir, John. *Our National Parks*. Boston: Houghton, Mifflin and Company, 1901.

Mumford, Lewis. "Tools Users vs. Homo Sapiens and the Megamachine." In *Philosophy of Technology*, ed. Robert C. Scharff and Cal Dusek, Malden, MA: Wiley Blackwell, 2014, 381–88.

Naess, Arne. "The Deep Ecological Movement: Some Philosophical Perspectives." *Philosophical Inquiry*, vol. 8, no. 102 (1986): 10–31.

Neiman, Susan. *Evil in Modern Thought: An Alternative History of Philosophy*. Princeton, NJ: Princeton University Press, 2004.

Nietzsche, Friedrich. *The Gay Science*. New York: Vintage, 1974.

Noonan, John T., Jr. *The Morality of Abortion: Legal and Historical Perspectives*. Cambridge, MA: Harvard University Press, 1970.

Oreskes, Naomi, and Erik M. Conway. *Merchants of Doubt: How a Handful of Scientists Obscured the Truth on Issues from Tobacco Smoke to Global Warming*. New York: Bloomsbury Press, 2011.

Osborne, Mark. "Judge throws out lawsuit filed by horse against former owner." *Yahoo! News*, 18 September, 2018.

Pack, Justin. *Amor Mundi and Overcoming Modern World Alienation*. Lanham, MD: Lexington Books, 2020.

Plant, Judith. "Feminism and Bioregionalism." In *Home! A Bioregional Reader*, ed. Van Andruss, Judith Plant, et al. Gabriola, BC: New Society Publishers, 1990: 21–23.

Pollan, Michael. *In Defense of Food: An Eater's Manifesto*. New York: Penguin, 2009.

Pope Francis. *Laudato Si': On Care for Our Common Home*. [Encyclical]. 2015.

Radford Reuther, Rosemary. *New Woman, New Earth: Sexist Ideologies and Human Liberation*. Boston, MA: Beacon Press, 1995.

Regan, Tom. *The Case for Animal Rights*. Berkeley, CA: University of California Press, 2004.

Ritzer, George. *The McDonaldization of Society*. Los Angeles, CA: SAGE, 2013.

Rorty, Richard. *Philosophy and the Mirror of Nature*. Princeton, NJ: Princeton University Press, 1981.

Ruddick, Sarah. *Maternal Thinking: Towards a Politics of Peace*. Boston, MA: Beacon Press, 1995.

Sahlins, Marshall. *Stone Age Economics*. Chicago, IL: Aldine-Atherton Inc., 1972.

Sale, Kirkpatrick. *Dwellers in the Land: A Bioregional Vision*. Athens, GA: University of Georgia Press, 2000.

Scott, James C. *Against the Grain: A Deep History of the Earliest States*. New Haven, CT: Yale University Press, 2017.

Sessions, George. "Ecocentrism, Wilderness and Global Systems Protection." In *The Wilderness Condition: Essays on Environment and Civilization*, ed. Max Oelschlaeger, Covelo, CA: Island Press, 1992, 90–130.

Shiva, Vandana. "Women's Indigenous Knowledge and Biodiversity Conservation." *India International Centre Quarterly*, vol. 19, nos. 1–2 (Spring–Summer 1992): 205–14.

Singer, Peter. *Animal Liberation*. New York: Harper, 2009.

Smith, Adam. *An Inquiry into the Nature and Causes of the Wealth of Nations*. London: W. Strahan and T. Cadell, 1776.

Sturgeon, Noel. "Naturalizing Race: Indigenous Women and White Goddesses." In *Environmental Philosophy: From Animal Rights to Radical Ecology*, 4th edition, ed. Michael Zimmerman et al., New York: Pearson, 2004, 228–51.

Talbot, Carl. "The Wilderness Narrative and the Cultural Logic of Capitalism." In *The Great New Wilderness Debate*, ed. J. Baird Callicot and Michael P. Nelson, Athens, GA: University of Georgia Press, 1998.

Taylor, Charles. *Philosophical Papers: Volume 2, Philosophy and The Human Sciences*. New York: Cambridge University Press, 1985.

———. *Sources of the Self: The Making of the Modern Identity*. Cambridge, MA: Harvard University Press, 1992.

Tucker, Robert C., ed. *The Marx–Engels Reader*. New York: W.W. Norton, 1978.

Turner, Cory. "Why Schools Fail to Teach Slavery's 'Hard History'." NPR, 4 February, 2018.

Wall Kimmerer, Robin. *Braiding Sweetgrass: Indigenous Wisdom, Scientific Knowledge and the Teaching of Plants*. Minneapolis, MN: Milkweed Editions, 2015.

———. *Gathering Moss: A Natural and Cultural History of Mosses*. Corvallis, OR: Oregon State University Press, 2003.

Warren, Mary Anne. "On the Moral and Legal Status of Abortion." *The Monist*, vol. 57, no. 1 (1973): 43–61.

White, Lynn, Jr. "The Historical Roots of Our Ecological Crisis." *Science*, vol. 155, no. 3767 (10 March 1967): 1204–05.

Wilson, Stephen. *The Magical Universe: Everyday Ritual and Magic in Pre-Modern Europe*. New York: Hambledon and London, 2000.

Woodward, Aylin. "Frogs are dying off at record rates—an ominous sign the 6th mass extinction is hitting one group of creatures hardest." *Business Insider*, 7 June, 2019.

INDEX

activism vs. theory, 13, 59–60, 97–98
Adams, Carol, 81, 100–01
alienated labor, 103–04, 161–62
    See also world alienation
American Transcendentalists, 118
amor fati, 164–65
amor mundi vs. world alienation, 31,
    164–66
anarchism, 92, 93–94
animal liberation
    background, 109–11
    animal ethics vs., 112
    animal rights vs., 112–13
    sixth mass extinction, 113–14
    See also climate change movement; food
        ethics
Animal Liberation (Singer), 109, 110–11,
    141, 158
anthropocentrism
    appeal of climate change movement,
        119–20
    ecocentrism and, 60, 65, 75–76
    economism, 145, 146, 150, 159
    Leopold's land ethic and, 69–70
    modernity and, 55
    as widespread and ingrained, 126, 140
    See also ecocentrism
appropriation, cultural, 20, 84–85
Arendt, Hannah, 35, 149, 153–56, 164
Aristotle, 146–47

Bacon, Francis, 148–49
banality of evil, 156
Bauman, Zygmunt, 141
Berry, Wendell, *Bringing It to the Table*, 103
Big Soldier (Osage chief), 48, 163
biophobia, 140–42, 158
bioregionalism
    characterized, 89–91
    activism vs. theory and, 60
    concerns about, 93–94
    dwelling in the land, 91–92
    local eating and living, 94
    politics of, 92
    radical homemaking, 93, 94
    See also deep ecology; ecocentrism;
        ecofeminism; place
Birch, Thomas, 74
Bonilla-Silva, Eduardo, 140
Brague, Rémi
    empirical understanding of the cosmos,
        31–32
    technology as morality, 37–38, 63–64
    Timaean Cosmos, 33
    See also Western perspectives
Bringing It to the Table (Berry), 103
Buddhism, 66

CAFOs (concentrated animal feed opera-
    tions), 104
capitalism, 130–32, 146–48
care ethics, 82–84

Carson, Rachel, *Silent Spring*, 118, 141, 158
The Case for Animal Rights (Regan), 112–13
Christianity, premodern, 51, 54–56
civilization vs. wilderness, 72
climate change movement
   climate change, characterized, 119–21
   environmentalism, antecedents to,
      117–18
   environmentalism, beginnings, 118–19
   getting involved, 121–22
   See also animal liberation; food ethics
climate denial
   introduced, 11–12, 125–26
   cigarette industry and, 129–30
   doubt-mongering, 132–33
   ethical and temporal registers, 134–35
   learned ignorance, 135–36
   market fundamentalism vs. regulation,
      130–32
   political polarization and lies, 133–34
   See also economism; epistemic igno-
      rance; thoughtlessness; world alien-
      ation
colonialism
   food production and, 106
   as modernization, 16
   wilderness debate and, 72–75
concentrated animal feed operation
   (CAFOs), 104
consumerism, 93
contemplation, 34–35
Conway, Erik, *Merchants of Doubt*, 126,
   129–35
cosmos
   contemplating, 34–35
   empirical understanding of, 31–32
   ethics and human nature in Timaean,
      33–34
   ethics for a new universe, 37–38
   metaphysical structure of, 32–33
   modern understanding of, 16–18
   replaced by the universe, 35–37
   See also Native American perspectives
creation stories, 21
cultural appropriation, 20, 84–85

Dawes Act (1877), 16
The Death of Nature (Merchant), 41
deep ecology
   activism vs. theory and, 6
   assessing, 75–76
   challenging economically-driven para-
      digms, 61–62

   ecocentrism and, 67
   principles of, 64–66
   seeking alternatives through, 63–64
   shallow vs., 61, 62–63
   spirituality, 66–67, 76
   See also bioregionalism; ecocentrism;
      ecofeminism
Della Porta, Giambattista, 42
Deloria, Vine, Jr.
   as academic and activist, 19–21
   colonial imposition of science, 56
   on ethics, 23
   Indigenous traditions, 27–28
   on "nature" and "Earth," 165–66
   on power and place, 21–23
   religion vs. science, 53
   on Western metaphysics and science,
      24–26
   on world alienation, 162–63
   See also Native American perspectives
Descartes, René, 37, 42
Devall, Bill, 61–62, 64, 66
difference feminism, 80–81, 84–85
disorder, nature as, 44–45
Dodge, Jim, 92
dominance critique, 81, 82–84
doubt-mongering, 132–33
dwelling in the land, 91–92

Earth alienation, 162, 165
ecocentrism
   activism vs. theory and, 60
   anthropocentrism and, 60, 65, 75–76
   assessing, 75–76
   deep ecology and, 67, 69
   Aldo Leopold and the land ethic, 69–70
   in practice, 70–72
   wilderness debate and colonialism, 72–75
   See also bioregionalism; deep ecology;
      ecofeminism
eco-fascism, 75
ecofeminism
   activism vs. theory and, 60
   against domination; toward care, 82–84
   criticisms of, 84–85
   feminisms, 79–81, 83
   masculine hyper-individualism, 41–42
   nature as female, 43–44
   nature as uncontrollable, 44–45
   standpoint theory, 81–82
   See also bioregionalism; deep ecology;
      ecocentrism
economic freedom, 130–32, 146–48

economism
    characterized, 145–48
    appeal of climate change movement,
        119–20
    moral appeal of, 150–51
    myth of progress, 146, 148–50
    See also climate denial; epistemic
        ignorance; thoughtlessness; world
        alienation
Eichmann, Adolf, 155–56
Eichmann in Jerusalem (Arendt), 156
Emerson, Ralph Waldo, 118
Enlightenment period, 118
environmental crisis(es)
    modern vs. premodern, 15–18
    rooted in premodern Christianity, 51,
        54–56
environmentalism
    antecedents to, 117–18
    beginnings of, 118–19
    climate denial and, 135–36
    See also animal liberation; climate
        change movement; food ethics
environmental theories. See bioregional-
    ism; deep ecology; ecocentrism; eco-
    feminism
epistemic ignorance
    militant ignorance, 137
    terracide without biophobia, 140–42
    white ignorance, 138–40
    See also climate denial; economism;
        thoughtlessness; world alienation
epistemic privilege, 81–82, 138
epistemology
    metaphysics vs., 52
    Native American, 22–23
equality feminism, 80–81
essentialism, 80–81, 85
Estabrook, Barry, 103–04
ethics
    animal liberation vs., 112
    in argumentation about climate change,
        134–35
    care ethics, 80, 82–84
    Christianity and science sharing funda-
        mental, 56–57
    land and sea ethics, 63
    Leopold's land ethic, 69–70
    Native American, 23–24
    for a new universe, 37–38
    Timaean Cosmos and, 33–34
    See also food ethics; morality
extinction, 113–14

The Faerie Queene (Spenser), 43
fallacy of misplaced concreteness, 25
farming and labor, 103–04
fast food, 105
feminism
    concerns about bioregionalism, 93–94
    types of, 79–81, 83
    See also ecofeminism
Food Chains (2014), 104
food ethics
    CAFOs, 104
    farming and labor, 103–04
    industrialization of eating, 101–02
    intersectionality and food, 105–06
    slow food, 104–05
    vegetarianism, 99–101
    See also animal liberation; climate
        change movement; ethics
food sovereignty, 106
Fox, Michael Allen, 100
Francis (pope), 56
Francis of Assisi, Saint, 56
Freedman, Milton, 130
freedom
    economic, 130–32, 146–48
    tied to science and technology, 149–50
free markets, 130–32, 146–48
From the Closed World to the Infinite Uni-
    verse (Koyre), 31

gender
    bioregionalism, concerns about, 93–94
    differences in moral reasoning, 80
    masculinity and meat-eating, 100
    nature as female, 43–45, 82–83
    See also ecofeminism
gendered violence, 41, 45
Gilligan, Carol, 80, 84
Guha, Ramachandra, 74

"The Historical Roots of Our Ecological
    Crisis" (White), 54
Hobbes, Thomas, 42
homemaking, 93, 94
Honoré, Carl, 105
The Human Condition (Arendt), 162

identity, modern, 150–51
ignorance, learned, 135–36
    See also epistemic ignorance
Indigenous technologies, 26
Indigenous traditions, 19, 27–28
    See also Native American perspectives

individualism, 41–42, 165
industrialization of eating, 101–03
industrio-scientific paradigm, 92–93
intersectionality, 60, 81, 85, 105–06
IPCC (Intergovernmental Panel on Climate Change), 11, 120

Jonas, Hans, 35–36, 46–47, 135

Kant, Emmanuel, 112–13, 138
Kimmerer, Robin Wall, 23–24, 163
Kittay, Eva, 79, 81
Kolbert, Elizabeth, 114
kosmos, 16
Koyre, Alexandre, From the Closed World to the Infinite Universe, 31

labor, alienated, 103–04, 161–62
land and sea ethics, 63
land ethic, Aldo Leopold's, 67, 69–70
learned ignorance, 135–36
Leaves of Grass (Whitman), 118
Leibniz, Gottfried Wilhelm, 54
Leopold, Aldo, 67, 69–70, 118
Lessler, Faye, 121
The Life of the Mind (Arendt), 154, 158
local eating and living, 94
Love's Labor (Kittay), 79

Machiavelli, Niccolò, 44
machine, nature as, 45–46, 82–83
"The Madman" (Nietzsche), 47
market fundamentalism vs. regulation, 130–34
Marx, Karl, 81, 103, 161
Marxist feminism, 83
masculinity
    hyper-individualism and, 41–42
    meat-eating and, 100
    toxic, 83–84, 100
mass extinction, 113–14
Maternal Thinking (Ruddick), 84
Menger, Carl, 147
Merchant, Carolyn
    death of nature, 46–47, 82–83
    Earth as machine, 17, 45–46
    gendered violence, 45
    nature as female, 43–44
    world as interconnected organism, 41–42
    See also nature
Merchants of Doubt (Oreskes and Conway), 126, 129–35

Mesthene, Emmanuel, 149–50
metaphysics
    epistemology vs., 52
    Native American, 21–22
    structure of the cosmos, 32–33
    Western science and, 24–26
Milgram, Stanley, 156–57
Mills, Charles, 126, 137–40
Milton, John, Paradise Lost, 43
misinformation, 11–12
modernity
    characterized, 15–16
    anthropocentrism and, 55
    colonialism, 16
    cosmos, modern understanding of, 16–18
    death of nature, 46–47
    fragmentation of human acts, 157
    gendered violence in, 41
    mechanical order, 45–46
    modern morality, 37–38, 63–64
    as progress, 47–49
morality
    gender differences in reasoning, 80
    immorality of seemingly innocuous actions, 141
    place and, 26–27
    technology as form of, 37–38, 63–64
    Timaean Cosmos and, 23–34
    See also ethics
Mother Earth, concept of, 43–45, 47, 82–83
movements, environmental. See animal liberation; climate change movement; food ethics
movements vs. theories, 13, 59–60, 97–98
Muir, John, 69, 72, 118

Naess, Arne, 62–63, 64–66, 75–76, 148
Native American perspectives
    deep ecology and, 64
    Vine Deloria Jr., work of, 19–21
    epistemology, 22–23
    ethics, 23–24
    Indigenous traditions, 19, 27–28
    metaphysics, 21–22
    Western metaphysics and science, 24–26
    Western technology, 26–27
    world alienation and, 162–63
nature
    death of, 46–47, 82–83
    Vine Deloria Jr. on concept of, 165–66
    as disorder, 44–45
    domination of as spiritual, 51, 54–56

as female, 43–45, 82–83
mechanical order, 45–46
progress and, 47–49
technology used to tame, 37
the world as organism, 41–43
Nietzsche, Friedrich, 36, 47, 164
Noonan, John, 109

Oreskes, Naomi, *Merchants of Doubt*, 126,
    129–35

paganism, struggle against, 45, 54–55, 83
Paradise Lost (Milton), 43
Paris Agreement (2015), 120
Pascal, Blaise, 35–36
Pinchot, Gifford, 118
place, 21–23, 26–27
    See also bioregionalism
Plant, Judith, 93
platform of deep ecology, 64–66
Plato, 33–34, 147
Plotinus, 34
political polarization, 133–34
Pollan, Michael, 101–02
pollution management, 62
positivism, 53
postcolonial feminism, 83
postcolonialism, 73
power and place, 21–23, 26–27
Power and Place (Deloria and Wildcat), 20
progress
    modernity as, 47–49
    myths of, 146, 148–50
    See also economism
prophecy of doom vs. prophecy of bliss,
    135

The Racial Contract (Mills), 139
radical homemaking, 93, 94
rape, 43, 45, 83
Red Alert! (Wildcat), 28
reformist environmentalism, 62
Regan, Tom, *The Case for Animal Rights*,
    112–13
regulation vs. market fundamentalism,
    130–34
religion
    implications of, 56–57
    roots of environmental crisis, 54–56
    science vs., 52–54
residential schools, 16, 25
resource management, 62
resources for getting involved, 121–22

Ritzer, George, 105
Romanticism, 72, 117–18
Roosevelt, Theodore, 118
Ruddick, Sarah, *Maternal Thinking*, 84

Salatin, Joel, 103
Sale, Kirkpatrick, 91–92
A Sand County Almanac (Leopold), 69
science
    alignment with Christianity, 56–57
    anti-regulation sentiments, 130–32
    freedom tied to, 149–50
    limits of, 24–26, 27, 53
    as predatory and abusive, 25–26
    religion vs., 52–54
Seitz, Fred, 129–32
Seneca, Lucius Annaeus, 34
Sessions, George, 71
sexualized language, 45, 46, 83
Shiva, Vandana, 82
Sierra Club, 118
Silent Spring (Carson), 118, 141, 158
Singer, Fred, 129–32
Singer, Peter, *Animal Liberation*, 109,
    110–11, 141, 158
sixth mass extinction, 113–14
slow food, 104–05
Smith, Adam, 147
speciesism, 109, 111
Spenser, Edmund, *The Faerie Queene*, 43
spirituality, 24–25, 53, 57, 66–67, 76
standpoint theory, 81–82, 138
Sturgeon, Noel, 84–85

Talbot, Carl, 73
Taylor, Charles, 142, 150–51
technology
    alignment with Christianity, 56–57
    Francis Bacon on, 148–49
    as form of morality, 37–38, 63–64
    freedom tied to, 149–50
    preserving American democracy,
        130–31
    in reformist environmentalism, 62
    taming nature, 37
    Western, 26–27
terracide, 140–42, 158
theories, environmental. See bioregional-
    ism; deep ecology; ecocentrism; eco-
    feminism
theory vs. activism, 13, 59–60, 97–98
Thoreau, Henry David, 69, 118

thoughtlessness
  Arendt on thinking and, 153–55
  Eichmann and thoughtless cognition,
    155–56
  environmental crisis, implications on,
    158–59
  Milgram's shock box, 156–57
  See also climate denial; economism;
    epistemic ignorance; world alien-
    ation
Thunberg, Greta, 120
Timaean Cosmos, 33–34
toxic masculinity, 83–84, 100

universe
  birth of, and death of the cosmos, 35–37
  ethics for a new, 37–38
  living cosmos vs., 17
  as personal, 21
unum versum (universe), 17
utilitarianism, 110–11

vegetarianism, 99–101

Walden (Thoreau), 118
Warren, Mary Anne, 109–10
Watson, Bob, 113
Western perspectives
  contemplating the cosmos, 34–35
  ethics for a new universe, 37–38
  metaphysical structure of the cosmos,
    32–33
  metaphysics and science, 24–26
  organic unity, 41–42

technology, 26–27
Timaean Cosmos, 33–34
universe and death of cosmos, 35–37
We Talk, You Listen (Deloria), 19
White, Lynn, Jr., 54–57
  See also religion
white ignorance, 138–40
Whitman, Walt, Leaves of Grass, 118
Wildcat, Daniel
  on alienation, 164
  colonial imposition of science, 56
  power and place, 21–23
  Power and Place, 20
  Red Alert!, 28
  technology and moral losses, 26–27
  on Western metaphysics and science,
    24–25
  See also Native American perspectives
wilderness debate and colonialism, 72–75
The Wisdom of the World (Brague), 31
witches, domination of, 45, 54–55, 83
world alienation
  characterized, 161–64
  alienated labor, 103–04, 161–62
  amor mundi, 31, 164–66
  desperate times, 166
  Earth alienation vs., 162, 165
  emancipation of the modern age and,
    149
  technology and, 26–27
  See also climate denial; economism;
    epistemic ignorance; thoughtless-
    ness

From the Publisher

A name never says it all, but the word "Broadview" expresses a good deal of the philosophy behind our company. We are open to a broad range of academic approaches and political viewpoints. We pay attention to the broad impact book publishing and book printing has in the wider world; for some years now we have used 100% recycled paper for most titles. Our publishing program is internationally oriented and broad-ranging. Our individual titles often appeal to a broad readership too; many are of interest as much to general readers as to academics and students.

Founded in 1985, Broadview remains a fully independent company owned by its shareholders—not an imprint or subsidiary of a larger multinational.

To order our books or obtain up-to-date information, please visit broadviewpress.com.

broadview press
www.broadviewpress.com

This book is made of paper from well-managed FSC® - certified
forests, recycled materials, and other controlled sources.